50 GREAT JUDO CHAMPIONS

50 GREAT JUDO CHAMPIONS

By
SIMON HICKS & NICOLAS SOAMES

IPPON BOOKS
A FIGHTING FILMS COMPANY

Ippon Books Ltd is a Fighting Films company

Fighting Films Ltd
1 Triangle House
2 Broomhill Road
London SW18 4HX
United Kingdom
Tel: +44 (0)20 8877 1441
Fax: +44 (0)20 8874 8590
www.fightingfilms.com
E-mail: info@fightingfilms.com

ISBN 1 8745729 1 7

Acknowledgements
With thanks to Katsuhiko Kashiwazaki, Alexander Iatskevich, Michel Brousse, Ulrich Klocke, Syd Hoare, Nicola Fairbrother, Shinji Inaba, Andrzej Sadej, Barnaby Chesterman, John Moon and Hans van Essen at Infostrada for their invaluable help in research.

Designed and Produced by ADS.
Printed by Bath Press Limited.

CONTENTS

Jigoro Kano.

Jean-Luc Rougé and Sumio Endo.

Hitoshi Saito and Angelo Parisi.

Ingrid Berghmans.

CONTENTS

Toshihiko Koga.

David Khakhaleichvili.

Cecille Nowak and Ryoko Tamura.

INTRODUCTION

Ki-Young Jeon and Marco Spittka.

WHAT ARE the qualities that make a champion?

Judo has produced many great champions in its exciting history and in choosing fifty of the greatest to date we have not only considered their competition records but also what they have contributed to the sport. Some were the greatest fighters, some the biggest personalities, and others continued to champion judo long after their competitive careers had passed.

Of the fifty champions we have chosen, we are sure that most would feature on everybody's list of the greatest. Inevitably, there will be some disagreement - for important figures we have omitted and for others whom we have included.We do not suggest that this is, in any way, a definitive list of the best champions that judo has produced. It is just our choice.

And, as you will see, the order in which they are presented is dictated solely by their dates of birth.

However, we hope that this book will help to keep alive memories of the great moments of our sport. Many of them are captured here in truly spectacular photographs, fleeting glimpses of victory and defeat. These are largely the work of the experienced judo photographers David Finch and Bob Willingham. And we are also very grateful for the contribution of Patrick Vial, who provided us with excellent, previously unpublished pictures of Okano, Fujii, and Endo; and the contribution of Colin McIver for his shots of Yamashita in action at the 1981 world championships.

We are sure that the following pages will inspire intense debate from the judo world. Who was the greatest at each weight? Who would have beaten whom had they fought each other at their best?

Imagine a heavyweight category containing Geesink, Ruska, Rouge, Endo, Parisi, Yamashita, Saito, Kakhaleichvili and Douillet. Who would defeat whom and who would emerge the winner? They are all here so this is the opportunity to compare their records and their techniques, and decide for yourselves.

Let us hope that the next fifty years of the International Judo Federation will prove as exciting as the first fifty which this book celebrates.

And that judo continues to produce champions as colourful, interesting, innovative and brilliant.

Simon Hicks and Nicolas Soames, June 2001

FOREWORD

Yong Sung Park, President IJF.

Seoul, 2001

ON JULY 12TH, 1951 nine countries met in a private room at Choy's Chinese restaurant in London to form the **International Judo Federation**. It was an historic moment for judo, demonstrating that an Eastern combat method had become a modern international sport. This was the beginning of the world judo movement, the start of the world judo championships, and a key step leading to the inclusion of judo in the Olympic programme.

This book is a celebration of the first 50 years of the IJF, and the 50 champions represent thousands of fantastic judokas, with their skills, their dedication, their professional preparation and their courage.

I was elected as the President of the International Judo Federation in 1995 and since then I have attended championships in all corners of the globe. I remain amazed at the quality and character of the fighters, both men and women, who attend the top competitions and compete for the highest honours.

Their successes allow them to return to their countries with medals. But equally important is that they have become heroes in their countries and international ambassadors for our sport, demonstrating the high standards expected on the mat. This brings judo to a wider public than ever before.

Now, judo is truly a world sport. At the Olympic Games, more countries participate at judo than in any other sport – a remarkable statistic.

We look forward to the next 50 years of international judo knowing that it will produce many more great champions. It is the inventiveness of so many of these champions that makes judo such a rich and ever-evolving sport.

Yong Sung Park
President of the International Judo Federation

Jigoro Kano and the early champions

JIGORO KANO, the founder of judo, was originally attracted to ju-jitsu in order to learn to defend himself against older students. The practice of ju-jitsu had declined so that it was the preserve, largely, of the rougher, tougher end of society. This is often mentioned in histories of Kano and it is easy to overlook the extraordinary fact that here was a highly educated teenager searching among the tough sections of Tokyo society for bona fide ju-jitsu teachers. Certainly Kano had the nature, the ambition and the fearlessness of a champion.

He learned first from Hachinosuke Fukuda, a man from a samurai background working in the ju-jitsu tradition; then Kano moved on to two other schools where he learned more tachi-waza and newaza. In 1882 at the age of just 22, (the same year that he was appointed lecturer in politics and economics at a leading private school for the nobility), he opened the Kodokan at Eishoji Temple. He had nine pupils.

Kano was aware of Western sports, and it was likely that this contributed to his view of the philosophical ideas behind the Kodokan. Judo, as he called his new form, should be concerned with the development of skills, of physical health, of education, and of character. Competition played a key role in all this. But he was concerned that

Shiro Saigo | Tsunejiro Tomita | Yoshiaki Yamashita | Sakujiro Yokoyama

safety should prevail: competiton was not simply about who could overcome all opponents no matter what injury was caused. Combat – in the right spirit – nurtured personal and technical progress. For Kano, competition really did promote 'mutual welfare and benefit'. This was one reason why rules were introduced right at the start of the Kodokan, allowing combat competition to take place in a more structured and protective environment.

His more educated environment certainly paid dividends. Within a year of its founding, the Kodokan moved to another district, where the rise in members required the mat area to extend from 12 to 20. In 1886, it moved again to a 40-mat tatami. It is interesting to note that by 1907, the membership of the Kodokan had risen to 10,000.

In the first years of its existence it attracted the curiosity and even ire of many other ju-jitsu schools. The Kodokan's reputation was established by competitions with other schools, which, according to Kodokan history, it won on virtually every occasion.

There are very few examples extant of Kano's own fighting skills. He must have been capable or he would not have attracted so many pupils so quickly. Kazuzo Kudo tells of Kano, in his early years as a ju-jitsu student, studying old ju-jitsu scrolls to throw a particularly tough opponent who always had beaten him. He came up with kata-guruma – which did the trick. There is also the story of Kano, on a ship, being challenged by a much larger Russian and throwing him with uki-goshi, his tokui-waza.

But the reputation of the Kodokan in those early years was upheld by the 'Four Heavenly Guardians' as they were called – Shiro Saigo, Tsunejiro Tomita, Yoshiaki Yamashita and Sakujiro Yokoyama. The turning point was the famous competition with ju-jitsu schools under the auspices of the Tokyo Metropolitan Police with the prize effectively being the licence to teach the police. Kodokan won all bouts with the exception of two that ended in a draw. It was this competition which saw Saigo, a small but hot-tempered man, win with his famous yama-arashi.

But all four were regularly present and effective when ju-jitsu fighters from other schools would turn up at the Kodokan – often unannounced – and issue a challenge. And for all Kano's insistence on a philosophical and ethical basis to the practice, confrontations could be harsh affairs.

In The Fighting Spirit of Japan (E.J. Harrison, Foulsham 1955) Sakujiro Yokoyama remembers some of those early fights – starting with the days before the foundation of the Kodokan. 'In those days contests were extremely rough and not infrequently cost the participants their lives. Thus, whenever I sallied forth to take part in one of these affairs, I invariably bade farewell to my parents since I had no assurance that I should ever return alive. Competitions were such a drastic nature that few tricks were barred and we did not hesitate to have recourse to the most dangerous methods in order to overcome an opponent. I have had experiences of this kind without number.'

Most lasted just three or four minutes. But Yokoyama goes on to recall one contest which lasted 55 minutes and only ended when the Chief of the Metropolitan Police stepped in to order the suspension of the match to prevent fatal injury to both.

He also remembers, during the early Kodokan days, being with Kyozo Mifune – later 10th dan and one of the great judo stylists – they dispatched a group of 13 toughs causing trouble in a restaurant. 'The affair was over in less than three minutes,' recounts Yokoyama.

By the start of the 20th century, the Kodokan was developing an international reputation. Yukio Tani went to the UK, and made a reputation as an unbeaten fighter taking on all-comers in the music halls – not something approved by Kano. However, eventually he was instrumental in setting up The Budokwai, with Gunji Koizumi in 1918 – the first club in Europe. Yoshiaki Yamashita, in 1903, was sent by Kano to the USA to introduce judo, and taught President Theodore Roosevelt.

Mitsuyo Maeda, born in 1878, joined the Kodokan in 1897. He went to the USA with Tomita, and had, it is said, some 2000 contests against all-comers and was never beaten. He settled in Brazil in 1915 and contributed to the growth of judo there. He died in 1941, never having returned to Japan. In short, the men who took judo around the world were tough and extremely capable.

Jigoro Kano's introduction of rules in those early days made committed competition without injury possible. Competition rules were developed and changed as the years passed, but the main principles of ippon through throws, holds and submissions have remained unchanged.

The All-Japan Championships started in 1930. By that time, the Olympic movement was firmly established, Kano himself being a leading member of the Japanese Olympic delegation. He clearly had an eye on international events, though for the moment the strength of judo was firmly with the founding country.

This was the environment that produced, arguably, the greatest judo champion of all time – Masahiko Kimura. Born in 1917 in Kumamoto, he won his first dan at 15. Even then he was doing, according to his autobiography, five hours practice a day – including 300 press-ups. He was second dan at 16 and third dan a year later. He gained his fourth dan shortly after by throwing three third dans and six fourth dans for ippon.

Still a teenager, his prowess began to be noticed. When he was 19 he lost a match for the last time – he only lost four judo contests in his whole career. Standing 1.70m and weighing 86kg, he was not physically formidable, but his determination and his severe training programme made him a fearsome opponent.

In 1937, at the age of 20, he won the All-Japan Championships for the first time. He won most of his fights with his favourite technique, osoto-gari, or with combinations including ouchi-gari, and his strong newaza.

The final was a 15 minute match to be settled by waza-ari or ippon with extra-time periods of 15 minutes if there was no clear winner. In the second period of extra time, both scored waza-ari, Kimura using ippon-seoi-nage – another of his favourite techniques, but was then caught with an uchimata.

After 40 minutes Kimura switched tactics, took his opponent to the ground and held him with kuzure-kami-shiho-gatame. He was totally exhausted, but before he went to sleep that night he did 500 press-ups, 1 km of bunny hops, and 500 makiwara strikes.

In the following year he extended his daily training routine from six to nine hours. He called it the 'Triple Effort'.

He won the All-Japan Championships in 1938, and again in 1939, though all the other leading contenders were trying to find a way to stop him. Often he faced much bigger men, but he never lost.

One of the keys to his continual success, he says, was his period of meditation where he learned not to be overjoyed by his victories, but to regard them steadily.

His training methods were extreme. He toughened his hands and wrists by striking the makiwara and thrusting his fingers into a bowl containing hot sand. He learned Shotokan and Gojin-ryu karate. Training at the Kodokan, he would throw 23 or 24 men in successive randori before feeling that was sufficient training for the day. Many of those at the receiving end of his osoto-gari had concussion after the practice with him.

In 1940, he participated in the Tenran Shiai in front of the Emperor, and won. Here, he describes the final.

I faced Ishikawa, 5th dan. He was taller and heavier than I, but I had beaten him twice by ippon within 2 or 3 minutes before. In those days, my main arsenals for shiai were tsuri-komi-goshi, ouchi-gari, ippon-seoi, okuri-ashi-barai (left and right), de-ashi-barai (left and right), ogoshi, harai-goshi, and osoto-gari. I applied, for example, osoto-gari in a different manner depending on whether the opponent was large or small, and whether the opponent used the left or right variation kumite. Therefore, I was able to adjust my technique to any type of opponent. Weakness can be turned into strength by research. Weakness and strength are not at opposing poles, but are adjacent to each other separated by a sheet of paper.

The final started. Ishikawa grabbed my back lapel with his right hand. He then pulled down his right elbow. I cut this grip by force. Next moment, I grabbed his left sleeve with my right hand, dropped my hip and initiated ippon-seoi. Ishikawa had anticipated this move, and had already bent his right knee. He hopped to my right side and evaded my ippon-seoi. But I watched how he hopped in this moment. The next attack method flashed in my head. He kept the hold of my back lapel. I attempted ippon-seoi again, but this time, I stepped in less than last time. He hopped again to evade the ippon-seoi. However, my right palm had been pressed on his right knee cap at the moment his total body weight got loaded onto his right leg. Using the rightward momentum he generated when he hopped to the right, I rolled him in the forward-rightward direction. I scored ippon at the 42 second mark.

(TRANSLATION BY P D E KING)

Masahiko Kimura

After the war, judo was forbidden until 1947. Yasuichi Matsumoto won the first All-Japan Championships – Kimura did not participate, though he beat Matsumoto twice in other events that year. In 1949, Kimura reached the final of the All-Japan Championships with ease. He faced Takahiko Ishikawa 6th dan and fought one of the hardest matches of his life. It was declared a draw after two periods of extra time.

In 1950, he became part of a professional judo circuit that alienated him from the central judo fraternity in Japan. Professional judo was against Kano's ethics, it was felt. The warring spirit within Kimura refused to accept it and he took the risk. The circuit was successful at the start – he won all his fights – but faded, and Kimura started another professional fighting career abroad. He took part in pro-wrestling bouts, in no-rules bouts, involving some highly dangerous and bloody combats.

In one of these encounters he faced Helio Gracie who had established a strong reputation in Brazil. Gracie challenged Kimura, and Kimura accepted. They fought in Sao Paulo in 1951. The rules were set by Gracie – neither throws nor holds counted. Only submissions or unconsciousness. The mat was so soft, according to Kimura, that although he threw Gracie a number of times, even with osoto-gari, he couldn't knock Gracie out. A film record exists of the fight and shows the result – Kimura threw Gracie with a superb osoto-gari, held him in kuzure-kami-shiho-gatame, and switched to ude-garami to end the fight (Gracie refused to submit but his corner threw a white towel on the mat).

At the age of 40, Masahiko Kimura was still fighting professionally and he remained outside the central judo environment for much of his life. He died in 1993. Indisputably a great champion, he was also a figure who declined to conform.

Kano's successors insisted that judo should not be drawn into the prize-fight arena though he could not deny that at the start the sheer ability of these judo and ju-jitsu fighters to cope with all-comers created a remarkable reputation for judo as self-defence.

The efforts of men such as Trevor Leggett in Britain, Minosuke Kawaishi in France, Eric Rahn and Alfred Rhode in Germany continued the practice established by Kano of championing judo itself. Champions are not only those who win in contests.

As a result of their persistent and intelligent efforts, judo took root in numerous countries and became a world sport. The foundation of the European Judo Union in 1948 led to the International Judo Federation being formed in 1951. This created the platform for international judo competitions.

The first European championships was held in 1951 in Paris (open weight but divided in brown belt, first dan, second dan, third dan and open); and the first world championships in Tokyo in 1956 which were open weight and grade events. Finally, in 1964 came its first appearance at the Olympic Games in Tokyo, and its full acceptance on the Olympic programme in 1972.

Judo had taken its place on the main platform of international sport.

*'The sport that won my heart.
The sport in which I got to know myself.'*

THE FIRST time the world sat up and really took notice of judo was when Anton Geesink, the six foot six Dutchman, won the Olympic Games in Tokyo in 1964. Up to then, it had operated on the fringes of sport, regarded as a Japanese activity. In Tokyo, the Japanese were expected to win, even though Geesink had won the world title three years before.

Fighting in the open category, Geesink made the early rounds look easy. In the opening pool, he beat Alan Petherbridge (Great Britain) and Akio Kaminaga (Japan) and while this created expectations, Kaminaga still went through to the next round. In the semi-final, Geesink beat Theodore Bronovskis (Australia) with a foot-sweep in twelve seconds.

In the final, as expected, he faced Kaminaga again. As hajime was called, both men flung their hands into the air – a memorable start to an historic fight. It is often forgotten that it wasn't over easily. Though Kaminaga was much smaller – he weighed 100kg against Geesink's 127kg, and was just under six feet – he was highly skilled. It took eight minutes for Geesink to wear him down, take him down to the ground, and hold him in kesa-gatame.

As the referee raised his hand for ippon, the Dutch supporters couldn't wait any longer, and one ran on to the mat. In a gesture that endeared Geesink to the Japanese for ever afterwards, he waved away his compatriot, and allowed his opponent time to recover himself with dignity.

It was the climax of an extraordinary career. Despite his size, Geesink was highly skilled. His tokui-waza at first was ashiwaza – in particular okuri-ashi-barai and de-ashi-barai, but after years of hard training routines (including many visits to Japan) he developed a world class sasae-tsuri-komi-ashi, as well as uchimata. In addition, he worked hard at ground-work, becoming known especially for sangaku-waza – both as a hold and a strangle.

Born in Utrecht, he started judo at the age of 14, and progressed

ANTON GEESINK

DOB **6 April 1934**
TOWN/COUNTRY **Utrecht, Netherlands**
WEIGHT **+80kg/Open; actual weight: 127kg**
HEIGHT **2.02m 6ft 6ins**
OCCUPATION **International Olympic Committee member**

BEST RESULTS

Olympic Games
Tokyo 1964 gold (Open)

World Championships
Tokyo 1956 bronze (Open)
Paris 1961 gold (Open)
Rio de Janeiro 1965 gold (+80kg)

European Championships
gold 21 times (1952-1964 and 1967)

National Dutch Championships
gold 21 times

FAVOURITE TECHNIQUES
Sasae-tsuri-komi-ashi, uchimata, ashiwaza, harai-goshi, osoto-gari, mune-gatame, kesa-gatame

PRINCIPAL PUBLICATIONS
My Championship Judo (Foulsham), Judo (Elsevier Sport)

quickly. By the time he retired after winning his second world title in Rio de Janeiro, he had become the most successful European in judo by far, with 21 national titles and 21 European titles (at a time when there were various grade categories).

Geesink won his first world title in Paris in 1961, throwing the reigning champion Koji Sone, with soto-maki-komi, then tani-otoshi, and finally holding him with mune-gatame.

He records that he didn't feel he had reached the pinnacle of his judo. 'I realised that my judo was not yet mature,' he recalled. ' In order to perfect my contest judo, to consolidate my top position, it was necessary for me to go further into newaza.' He practised in his home dojo for months, working on sangaku-waza; and in 1963 he went again to Japan for three months, training in the dojo of Tenri University, where the newaza was particularly strong. This, he feels, prepared him finally for the Tokyo Olympics.

After his retirement, he became an international ambassador for judo. In the following decades, he travelled the world as one of the most recognised figures in sports circles. He became the International Olympic Committee member for Holland (in Utrecht, he lives in Anton Geesink Strasse) but his first love has always been judo.

In *My Championship Judo* (Foulsham), which he wrote on his retirement, he reflected: 'I was only fourteen years old when I set foot on the judo mat for the first time. My introductory bow was a hasty nod, and I plunged into the fight with the impetuosity, the intrepidity and the recklessness peculiar to a boy of that age. When I now set foot on the mat, my bow is deeper; it no longer reflects haste, but respect. What a lot my great Japanese teachers taught me there on the mat.'

Paris 1961 World Championship Final. Geesink attacks Kaminaga with uchimata.

Olympic victory, Tokyo 1964. Geesink waves away a Dutch supporter at the point of victory.

WILHELM RUSKA

DOB **28 September 1940**
TOWN/COUNTRY **Edam, Netherlands**
WEIGHT **+93k/Open; actual weight 115k**
HEIGHT **1.90m 6ft 3ins**
OCCUPATION

BEST RESULTS

Olympic Games
Munich 1972 gold (+93kg)/gold (Open)

World Championships
Salt Lake City 1967 gold (+93kg)
Mexico City 1969 silver (+93kg)
Ludwigshafen 1971 gold (+93kg)

European Championships
Berlin 1965 bronze (+93kg - Amateur)/ silver (Open)
Luxembourg 1966 gold (+93kg)
Milan 1967 gold (+93kg)
Ostende 1969 gold (+93kg)/gold (Open)
Berlin 1970 silver (+93kg)/ silver (Open)
Gothenburg 1971 gold (+93kg)
The Hague 1972 gold (+93kg); gold (Open)

National Dutch Championships
gold 10 times

FAVOURITE TECHNIQUES
Osoto-gari, tai-otoshi, harai-goshi, yoko-shiho-gatame

World Championship Final 1967, Salt Lake City. Ruska attacks Maejima (Japan).

WILHELM RUSKA was the first man to win two Olympic gold medals. Ruska's international competitive career began in 1965 in the European championships in Berlin where he won a silver and a bronze in the Open and heavyweight categories respectively – competing in the 'amateur' section of the tournament (at the time the event was divided into 'amateurs' and 'instructors'). It was a significant moment for Dutch judo, because this muscular blonde Dutchman was already chasing the man who had, of course, inspired him – Anton Geesink. And as Geesink came to the end of his career after the European championships in 1967, Ruska was ready to take his place.

Ruska was a different kind of champion. He had started judo at the age of 20, and rose rapidly through the ranks, using a natural balance and an exceptionally strong physique, as well as a fiercely competitive nature. Relatively light for a heavyweight – at 110kg – and only 1.90m, Ruska looked very different to Geesink; and though he trained in Japan, he would never be regarded as quite the technician as his larger compatriot.

But he could certainly throw. Ruska developed a strong double-lapel grip, allowing him to attack with his three main techniques – osoto-gari, tai-otoshi, and harai-goshi – without warning. It was said that the finishing technique simply depended on the way his opponent crumbled. His power also made him dangerous on the ground – though not invincible.

In 1966 he won his first major title – the +93kg category at the European championships, in Luxembourg, the first of seven European titles he was to win. The following year, he won it again, in Milan – when Geesink won the Open and then retired. And when he took the world title in Salt Lake City in the same year, beating the Japanese Maejima in the final, he demonstrated he had admirably filled the boots of his illustrious predecessor.

Injury interfered with the next two years, until he emerged powerfully again in 1969, winning the European heavyweight and Open in Ostende. However, losses in the world championships in the same year, and in the European event in the following year, showed that he could be beaten.

But not at the Munich Olympics in 1972. He had got back his confidence by winning the heavyweight division in the world championships in Ludwigshafen and both the heavyweight and Open in the European championships on home ground in The Hague in May 1972, setting himself up perfectly for the Games.

And no one could stand in his way. When the buzzer went, he strode across the mat, grabbed two lapels, powered his way to a throw or hold, and moved on to the next opponent. A few experienced adversaries, such as Klaus Glahn (Germany) who had beaten him in the past, managed to hold him to a decision, but Ruska never looked in danger of losing in the heavyweight category. He met Glahn again in the final (when it was possible to win through the repechage and come back into the main event) and finished the fight quickly, with harai-goshi in 1 minute 43 seconds.

The Open category looked like going the same way, but Ruska experienced a slight blip. In the third round he was, totally unexpectedly, caught by Vitaly Kuznetsov with te-guruma for ippon. Now it was Ruska's turn to fight back to the final, which he did by beating Glahn and then Brondani of Italy with osoto-gari. And he polished off Kuznetsov on the ground with yoko-shiho-gatame – not wanting to risk being caught with another counter.

The judo event of the 1972 Olympics began and ended with Ruska, and his double success confirmed his decision to retire – but to retire from amateur competition only. He followed Geesink again in taking up a well-paid option to work the professional wrestling circuit in Japan, which he did with some success.

Later, Ruska wrote: 'The most important thing is the spirit of combat. If you are too spoiled by life you can never be strong. At the age of seven, I got up at 4am to help my mother (a cleaner). I used to fetch and carry forty-two pails of water for her. I didn't have shoes, only sabots. It was a time of difficulty, but it gave me a strong mentality and I learned to make the most of each instant in all the combats of my life.'

Ruska takes his second Olympic gold medal against Vitaly Kuznetsov (Soviet Union) with yoko-shiho-gatame. Munich 1972.

NOBUYUKI SATO

DOB **12 Jan 1944**

TOWN/COUNTRY **Hakodate, Hokkaido, Japan**

WEIGHT **-93kg/Open**

HEIGHT **1.78m 5ft 10ins**

OCCUPATION **Professor, physical education department, Tokai University, Japan**

BEST RESULTS

World Championships
Salt Lake City 1967 gold (-93kg)
Mexico City 1969 bronze (Open)
Lausanne 1973 gold (-93kg)
Ludwigshafen 1971 silver (-93kg)

All-Japan Championships
1974 gold (Open)

European Sambo Tournament
1972 gold

PRINCIPAL PUBLICATIONS
Best Judo - with Isao Inokuma (Kodansha)
Ashiwaza (Ippon Books)

IN JAPAN, during his competitive days in the late 1960s and 1970s, Nobuyuki Sato was known as 'Newaza Sato' for the very simple reason that everyone feared his ground-work. This was the case at both national and international level – though the methods of getting his opponent to the ground varied. In Japan, it was most likely to be ashiwaza; abroad, it was more often tai-otoshi. But the final result was invariably the same – osaekomi.

Kuzure-kami-shiho-gatame on K. Sato. All Japan Championships, 1968.

However, his judo career has been much more than just competition. For ten years, from 1976 to 1985, he was manager of the Japanese national team, a successful period for Japan with such outstanding champions as Yasuhiro Yamashita, Katsuhiko Kashiwazaki, Sumio Endo, Shinji Hosokawa, Nobutoshi Hikage and Hitoshi Saito. It was also a difficult period for Japan, for the rest of the judo world was fast catching up – yet under the leadership of Sato, Japan still managed, at many major tournaments, to take about half of the men's gold medals.

And following his resignation in 1985 – at the same time as his star protegé Yamashita retired – he became director of the IJF's education and diffusion committee. It is interesting to look at his personal competitive career with the perspective of his future work in management. Nobuyuki Sato was born in the northern Japanese island of Hokkaido, and at 12, followed his brother Nobuhiro into judo: 'I loved fighting!' His brother was effectively his first teacher. An affinity for newaza showed itself early, but after an initial study of osoto-gari, he started working on ashiwaza. Sasae-tsuri-komi-ashi came first, then harai-tsuri-komi-ashi, and then other foot-sweeps.

When he went to Tsukuba University in the early 1960s, he began to make his mark in national events, aiming always at the All-Japan Championships, Japan's blue riband event, even though it was an Open category event, and at 84kg, he was often the lightest competitor. In 1966 he won a silver, and the following year another, losing only to Okano.

His international career beckoned, and he took heed of astute advice from Akio Kaminaga. 'He told me that because westerners adopt a wide stance I would find my ashiwaza difficult against them, and I should develop tai-otoshi,' recalls Sato. In 1967 he won his first world title, the -93kg category in Salt Lake City – throwing most opponents with tai-otoshi, and then holding them down. He won a bronze in the world Open category in Mexico City, beaten only by Wilhelm Ruska, and a silver at -93kg in Ludwigshafen. In the world championships in Lausanne, in 1973, he won again.

But time was passing, and his single goal of the All-Japan title seemed to be eluding him. His last chance came at the age of 30, in 1974, and, despite suffering badly from a cold, he won. 'If you set your mind to something, you can do it,' he told his pupil Kashiwazaki.

His retirement enabled him to concentrate on the judo department at Tokai University where he has taught since 1969 – he is still professor there. Over three decades he built it into one of the great powerhouses of Japanese universities, and has entertained numerous foreign teams throughout that period.

Osoto-gari on Ueno. All Japan Championships, 1968.

ISAO OKANO

DOB **20 January 1944**
TOWN/COUNTRY **Ibaragi Prefecture, Japan**
WEIGHT **-80kg**
OCCUPATION **Professor of judo**

BEST RESULTS

Olympic Games
Tokyo 1964 gold

World Championships
Rio de Janeiro 1965 gold

All-Japan Championships
1967 gold
1969 gold

FAVOURITE TECHNIQUES
Ippon-seoi-nage, kouchi-gari, yoko-shiho-gatame, shimewaza

THE JUDO of Isao Okano has been described as 'miracle' judo. Though he weighed around 80kg, his exceptional natural talent brought him gold medals in all the major national and international tournaments, including open-weight competitions.

He was, arguably, the most spectacular individual at the inaugural Olympic judo competition in Tokyo in 1964, producing stunning throws and a famous strangle – from underneath. Lionel Grossmain (France) couldn't believe it when he found himself on top of Okano in a hold. But the Japanese champion had purposely turned him into an unusual okuri-eri-jime, and after a few seconds the lights went out for the Frenchman – and Okano then used katsu on his hapless opponent to bring him round.

He was known particularly for seoi-nage and kouchi-gari, both of which were fast and precise. And it was with these, among other techniques, that he won the All-Japan championships (the open-weight event) as well as the national weight category championships, at the same time as establishing himself abroad.

His spectacular semi-final win over Hi Tai Kim (Korea) at the world championships in Rio de Janeiro in 1967, was typical of Okano at his prime. The competition area was a raised mat – as was customary in those days. It was the rule that if the opponent was thrown outside the area, no score was given. Okano spun in at full speed for seoi-nage but found, as he was about to throw, that he was right on the edge of the mat, and that Kim would land out of the area. Okano hesitated for a fraction of a second, facing the edge with Kim – who was a highly experienced fighter – and then spun again to throw Kim perfectly on his back inside the mat.

Okano attacks at the 1964 Olympics.

After his retirement, Okano became manager of the Japanese national team. His tenure, from 1972 to the Montreal Olympic Games in 1976, saw one of their most successful periods – in the world championships in Lausanne, 1973, the Japanese team secured the distinction for the last time of winning every category.

Widely known as a severe trainer who pushed his squad to the limits, Okano was concerned to foster judo for men of all nations. He founded the Seiki Juku, a school which attracted a strong international contingent.

In *Vital Judo – Throwing Techniques* (Japan Publications Inc 1973) written with Tetsuya Sato, Okano broke away from the format of most traditional judo books to consider what actually works during a judo competition. It is a revolutonary book, even today. In it, he comments:

'The only proper attitude is the willpower to perfect your abilities and to attain the goal you have set for yourself. Instead of finding satisfaction in past achievements, inspire yourself with the enthusiasm and fervour to go on to still greater achievements.

'I know that some men attempt to sidestep the issue of responsibility involved in winning and losing by saying that it is all a matter of luck. But anyone who entertains this attitude is already disqualified for consideration as a true judo winner. A person who lacks the willpower to look extreme difficulties in the face has no luck. Luck does not wait for one: one must make one's luck.'

He also wrote:

'Having given my entire youth to judo, the question of why I pour my whole mind and body into this martial art is a matter of the greatest importance to me. Moreover, since I intend to remain devoted to judo for the rest of my life, this question will probably retain its significance for me until the end. My fundamental answer to the question is this: ' In judo, I find the true essence of human life.'

JEAN-LUC ROUGÉ

DOB **30 May, 1949**
TOWN/COUNTRY **Gif-sur-Yvette, Chevreuse, France**
WEIGHT **-93kg/+95kg**
HEIGHT **1.93m 6ft 4 ins**
OCCUPATION **Director, French Judo Federation**

BEST RESULTS

World Championships
Vienna 1975 gold (-93kg)
Paris 1979 silver (+95kg)/bronze (open)

European Championships
Madrid 1973 gold (u93kg)
Lyons 1975 silver (-93kg)
Ludwigshafen 1977 gold (+95kg)
Helsinki 1978 bronze (+95kg)/bronze (open)
Brussels 1979 gold (+95kg)
Vienna 1980 gold (+95kg)

Tournoi de Paris
1974 gold (-93kg)
1976 silver (-93kg)
1977 gold (+95kg)
1979 gold (-95kg)

French National Championships
1969, 1973, 1975 (u93kg) gold
1976, 1977 (+95kg) gold
1971-74 (Open) gold

European Junior Champion
Berlin 1969 gold

European Espoir Championships
Lisbon 1967 gold

FAVOURITE TECHNIQUES
Osoto-gari, harai-goshi, uchimata

PRINCIPAL PUBLICATIONS
Harai-Goshi (Ippon Books)
Le Judo de Champion (Ichiban)

AS TECHNICAL director and then the director of the French Judo Federation over the past decade, Jean-Luc Rougé has played a key role in the growth of the sport in his homeland. He has helped France developed the largest judo population of any country outside Japan – a considerable achievement.

He has brought to judo administration the same Gallic passion and commitment he gave to his competitive career, which he crowned, in 1975, by winning the world light heavyweight title, the first time ever by a Frenchman. Other French Olympic and world gold medallists have followed him, but the fact that he opened the door first makes him one of the most prominent figures in judo to this day.

Rougé's style was always characterised by boldness. He used his height to his advantage, his long legs reaching for osoto-gari or ouchi-gari, which he brought off partly with skill and partly with his deceptive strength. But he was best-known for his harai-goshi, a technique for which he was perfectly built.

When he began judo at the age of 13, in a small town in the French countryside, he learned harai-goshi both to the left and right, and it was symptomatic of Rougé's extrovert nature that he attacked both sides with abandon at all levels of competition – using a double-lapel grip. His natural flair took him through the junior ranks – he developed his all-attacking style with a constant change of grips, of angles of attack, and of defence. On one occasion he said that if an opponent attacked with the same throw, he never defended the same way twice – once he would block, another time step round, a third time counter.

This unpredictability was very much part of his armoury. It was out of a flurry, in the semi-final of the -93kg category of the European championships in 1973 in Madrid, that the winning ashi-guruma appeared, to throw Muzaev of the Soviet Union; and it was the same all-action attacking that brought him the gold medal against the tough David Starbrook (Britain).

Two years later, in the world championships in Vienna, he won two fights with harai-goshi, throwing Ishibashi (Japan) in the final for the winning yuko with it. He won three further European titles in 1977, 1979 and 1980, but this time at heavyweight, before retiring.

Although he was a remarkably versatile fighter for so tall a man, he will always be remembered for a spectacular spin-turn harai-goshi, which saw him literally leap into the air, spin, and surprise his opponent by landing in the perfect position to sweep the loins. 'I knew it was a risky move, but I also knew that once I had launched it, it was quite difficult to stop.'

A spectacular harai-goshi against Muzaev (URS), typical of Rougé's attacking flair.

Rougé attacks Dave Starbrook (GBR) with kani-basami before the technique was banned. Rougé campaigned for its retention.

SHOZO FUJII

DOB **11 May 1950**

TOWN/COUNTRY **Oochi cho, Ookawa gun, Japan**

WEIGHT **-80kg / -78kg**

HEIGHT **1.70m 5ft 7ins**

OCCUPATION **Physical education teacher at Tenri University**

BEST RESULTS

World Championships
Ludwigshafen 1971 gold
Lausanne 1973 gold
Vienna 1975 gold
Paris 1979 gold

Asian Championships
Seoul 1974 gold (-80kg)/gold (Open weight)

Tournoi de Paris
1971 gold

Kano Cup
1978 gold

FAVOURITE TECHNIQUES
Morote-seoi-nage, tomoe-nage

SHOZO FUJII never wanted to be a judo player. All his boyhood heroes were sumo fighters and Shozo wanted to be one of the big men. At 12 he started judo as the way to becoming a sumotori, but within two months he had progressed so rapidly he was able to fight in his first tournament.

He loved the thrill of competition, and became a member of his middle school judo team. He progressed to Tenri High School and ultimately to Tenri University, winning the All-Japan junior championships at 19.

By now he realised he would never be big enough for a sumotori, and settled for judo, where he could fight in his weight-category, as well as the open weight. His first international tournament came in 1971, aged 20, at the first Tournoi de Paris. He was the star of the show, dazzling the knowledgeable French audience with superb skills, and winning with ease.

The same year he fought in his first world championships, in Ludwigshafen, Germany. He took the title, defeating his countryman Masashiga Shigematsu in the final and set his sights on the Olympic title in Munich the following year. But competition in Japan was fierce. Fujii remembers: 'When I was fighting it was more difficult to win the qualification tournaments in Japan than it was to win the world or Olympic Championships. Once I had qualified I could relax!' Only one fighter per country in each weight was allowed in the Olympics, and the spot was taken by Shinobu Sekine, who won the gold medal.

At home Fujii fought in the open weight of the All-Japan student championships, losing the final to Haruki Uemura, thirty kilograms heavier than himself. He would take the world open weight title in 1975 and the Olympic title in 1976. But it was a defeat Fujii remembers as one of the worst in his career. Proving himself against the big men, he came up against Uemura again in the All-Japan championships, losing in the semi-final and taking third place.

Indeed, for Fujii his most memorable contests were largely in open weight competition, in particular he believes one of his finest moments was beating the 1979 world open weight champion Sumio Endo to win the Asian Championships! In his weight Isamu Sonoda was his toughest opponent. The two of them met in the final of the 1973 Lausanne world championships, when Fujii took his second title.

In 1975, in Vienna, he took an unprecedented third world title, defeating another Japanese fighter, Yoshimi Hara, in the final with tomoe-nage, and was at the height of his powers. His principal technique at high school was uchimata, but now he threw everyone with his morote-seoi-nage, dropping to catch his opponent on his back, and then rising to unload him, even taking a few running steps before the huge ippon. This was his tokui-waza. He loved it because he was short, and it was the fastest, most spectacular route to an ippon! As the 1976 Olympics approached, Fujii, three times world champion, was the favourite to take the title.

It is his greatest regret that he badly injured his elbow before the Japanese trials for Montreal and, unable to use his morote-seoi-nage, lost his place to Isamu Sonoda, whom he had beaten in the 1973 world championships. Sonoda took the Olympic title, and Fujii had to re-think his judo. Unable to rely on his tokui-waza, he developed his secondary technique. Before long he was throwing regularly with tomoe-nage. Fujii's version was a classic, 'falling directly backwards' throw, but using two feet instead of one. The grip was the same as for his diminished seoi-nage, giving him greater attacking options.

In 1977 the IJF cancelled the world championships, when the hosts, Spain, refused to issue visas to Taiwan. It was four years before Fujii could defend his title again. By now, each country could send only one fighter to the worlds and, in Paris, Fujii was Japan's representative at -78kg. Using tomoe-nage, he reached the final, against home favourite, Bernard Tchoullouyan. Despite fervent crowd support for the Frenchman, in the most memorable fight of his life, Fujii took his fourth world title.

Yet he never appeared on an Olympic mat: the next year Japan boycotted the Moscow Games, and Fujii's magnificent career as a fighter was over. He served as one of Japan's national coaches, before becoming head coach at his alma mater, Tenri University.

He also became one of Japan's top referees, and found the pressures of refereeing greater than those being a fighter: 'As a fighter I was responsible only to myself; as a referee I am responsible to everyone else. If I ever make a big mistake I will stop refereeing.'

Shozo Fujii continues to coach at Tenri, an occupation he finds more satisfying than refereeing: 'I have learned a great deal from judo and I owe it a lot. I want to contribute to judo by teaching and setting a good example to my students, to whom I can teach judo as I feel it should be.' In his free time he still goes to the great Sumo bashos. Asked how he would fancy his chances against the huge Akebono he replys: 'In sumo I might lose, but put a judo jacket on him and I would win.'

The Fujii seoi-nage in action. 1975 World Championships, Vienna.

Fujii wins his fourth world title. Paris 1979.

SUMIO ENDO was one of the most unusual of Japanese heavyweight champions. He was remarkably short for a heavyweight, and one of the most visually memorable fights of his career was in the world championhips in Vienna, 1975, when he faced Jon-Gil Park of North Korea. Park was over 2 metres tall – nearly seven feet – weighed 150kg, and was a competent judoka. But Endo brought the spectators to their feet with a stunning ippon-seoi-nage for ippon.

Speed, allied to his low centre of gravity, was Endo's great asset. In sprint training, he was exceptionally fast off the starting blocks, and this could be seen on the mat. His upper body strength and gripping also made an impression on everyone he fought. In Japanese dojos, after randori, when the ropes came down, Endo could be seen hauling himself up to the roof on two ropes just using his hands – a rare ability for a heavyweight.

But underpinning all these physical attributes was a very wide technical range. Though ippon-seoi-nage was his tokui-waza, he was often seen executing harai-goshi (generally regarded a technique for a tall man) uchimata, and makikomi of various descriptions.

He burst on the international scene in 1974 at the Tournoi de Paris, winning comfortably and endearing himself forever to the French crowd. The next year, he scooped the world heavyweight title in Vienna, throwing Serge Novikov of the Soviet Union. But caution got the better of him in the Montreal Olympics and he lost to Novikov on that occasion by a decision.

Three years later, he won the world title for a second time, beating another top Russian, Vitali Kuznetsov with harai-makikomi. Despite being considerably smaller, he was able to use the winding element of the throw to good effect.

SUMIO ENDO

DOB **3 October 1950**

TOWN/COUNTRY **Koriyama City, Japan**

WEIGHT **+93kg; actual weight 259 pounds**

HEIGHT **1.69m 5ft 6.5ins**

OCCUPATION **Professor of Judo, Akitakeizhaihoka University**

BEST RESULTS

Olympic Games
Montreal 1976 bronze

World Championships
Vienna 1975 gold (+93kg)
Paris 1979 gold (Open)

Tournoi de Paris
1974 gold

All Japan Championships
1976 gold

Asian Championships
Seoul 1974 gold (+93kg)/silver (open)

FAVOURITE TECHNIQUES
Ippon-seoi-nage, harai-goshi, harai-makikomi, uchimata, uchimata-makikomi, kosoto-gari, suku-nage, uranage

Ippon seoi-nage. World Championships, Paris 1979.

Endo consistently demonstrated that judo techniques can be adapted to suit any physical shape, so long as the will to master them is there. In the same event he produced ippon scores with ippon-seoi-nage and tani-otoshi – the latter against the lanky Jean-Luc Rouge of France. He also threw Mohammed Rashwan, the capable Egyptian, who was over six feet tall. The throw was uchimata!

Fighting for the police section, the Keishicho, Endo was a familiar face in the pinnacle of Japanese tournaments, the All-Japan championships, throughout the 1970s. He won it in 1976, but while still at his peak he faced the rising talent of Yasuhiro Yamashita, who threw him with uchimata or held him down on their various encounters. However, in 1980, Endo tried a new tactic – kani-basami – in the course of which Yamashita suffered a serious leg injury. The fight was settled as a draw, but it led to the eventual international ban of the technique.

Always popular in the West, Endo has toured Europe teaching and giving demonstrations. On many occasions, a hapless uke has picked himself off the mat after a demonstration of ippon-seoi-nage, convinced he has never in his life been thrown so hard, in randori or competition.

Endo wins the 1979 world title.

Maki-komi. Japanese University Championships. Osaka 1972.

KATSUHIKO KASHIWAZAKI

DOB **16 September 1951**
TOWN/COUNTRY **Iwate Prefecture, Japan**
WEIGHT **-60kg/-65kg**
HEIGHT **1.70m 5ft 7ins**
OCCUPATION **Professor, International Budo University, Katsuura, Japan**

BEST RESULTS

World Championships
Vienna 1975 silver (-60kg)
Maastricht 1981 gold (-65kg)

All-Japan Weight Category Championships
1975, 1978, 1979, 1980, 1981 gold

World Sambo Championship
Bakul 1975 gold

FAVOURITE TECHNIQUES
Tomoe-nage, ouchi-gari, kosoto-gari, obi-tori-gaeshi, tate-shiho-gatame, yoko-shiho-gatame, shimewaza

PRINCIPAL PUBLICATIONS
Fighting Judo, with Terence Donovan (Pelham Books)
Tomoe-Nage, Shimewaza, Osaekomi, Attacking Judo (with Hidetoshi Nakanishi) all for Ippon Books
Newaza of Kashiwazaki (Baseball Magazine)

MOST JAPANESE world and Olympic champions show their talent early. Katsuhiko Kashiwazaki, world champion and five times Japanese champion, was an exception. When he arrived at Tokai University as a teenager, he was ranked about 16th of the 20 students of that year, and it was some time before he began to show real promise – the fruit of a total dedication, a fixed determination, and an imagination for technical innovation.

As in most top university dojos, every day starts with an early morning run. For the whole of his four years at Tokai, Kashiwazaki made sure he came first every day. He never allowed himself to be beaten. It was this that first made Tokai judo teacher Nobuyuki Sato first notice him.

Having broken his arm when 16, he could no longer do his favourite technique, morote-seoi-nage, and had to re-think his judo. He studied newaza, and eventually became so strong that by his fourth year at Tokai, he was part of the team in open-weight events, knowing how to keep big men at bay, and how to take them down and finish them on the ground. It was while at Tokai that he developed his facility with tomoe-nage and obi-tori-gaeshi, the latter widely regarded as merely a take-down, but which he developed into a fearsome technique.

Also, to broaden his fighting repertoire, he studied sambo (winning a world sambo title) and other non-Japanese forms of wrestling. He travelled to many countries, from Mongolia and the USSR to Europe.

Kashiwazaki graduated from Tokai at the age of 23, and became a teacher in Ibaragi prefecture in the north of Japan. He was national champion and heading for the Moscow Olympics, but insisted on the unusual route of being a full-time teacher, doing his personal training outside school hours.

He won a silver medal at the world championships in 1975 at -60kg, losing only to Yoshiharu Minami (at the time, two from each country were allowed to participate). His principal dream was to win the Olympic Games, and in the late 1970s he was still on course, being the No 1 -65kg fighter in Japan. In March, 1980, however, politics intervened, and Japan, along with the USA, pulled out of the Moscow Games. It was Kashiwazaki's greatest disappointment, but he maintained his form to win the world title in 1981, in Maastricht, Holland.

In the final, against Constantin Nicolae of Romania, he gave a superb display of his judo, throwing with furiko-tomoe-nage (pendulum tomoe-nage) and then holding him with yoko-shiho-gatame for ippon.

1981 World Championships, Maastricht. Throwing Thorsten Reissmann (East Germany) with a remarkable uchimata sukashi.

All his life, he had believed, and trained, that there should be no separation between tachi-waza and newaza, and in winning his world title, he demonstrated this clearly.

He won the Kano Cup the following year, and then retired. He was 31, relatively old for a lightweight. He stayed in England for a year, teaching at The Budokwai and learning English. On his return to Japan, he founded the judo section at the International Budo University at Katsuura, where he is now.

In addition to his competition successes, Kashiwazaki has always maintained a strong academic interest in judo. He has contributed regularly to Kindai Judo, and other leading Japanese judo journals. With the distinguished photographer Terence Donovan, he produced the book Fighting Judo. He was the author of three volumes in the Ippon Books Masterclass series: Tomoe-Nage, Shimewaza and Osaekomi. This, with his regular trips to teach around the world, has made him a well-known figure in many countries, and an inspiration to many, inside and outside Japan.

In the preface to Fighting Judo, Nobuyuki Sato, for 10 years team manager of the Japanese national judo squad, wrote:

'It has been said of Kashiwazaki and his judo that he is "a man who created art from effort." If I can make a comparison between Kashiwazaki and Yasuhiro Yamashita: the latter is an exemplary product of a system designed to create judo champions. He was nurtured by that system as a prize flower cultivated in a garden. Kashiwazaki, on the other hand, is like a wild flower which sprang up among weeds, training as he did in the country in northern Japan, whilst teaching in high school.'

VLADIMIR NEVZEROV

DOB **15 October 1952**
TOWN/COUNTRY **Majkop, Soviet Union**
WEIGHT **-70kg**
OCCUPATION **Care worker**

BEST RESULTS

Olympic Games
Montreal 1976 gold

World Championships
Vienna 1975 gold

European Championships
Lyons 1975 gold
Ludwigshafen 1977 gold

FAVOURITE TECHNIQUES
Tai-otoshi, ippon-seoi-nage (left and right), osoto-gari, uchimata, ashiwaza

VLADIMIR NEVZEROV was the first Russian – or fighter from any state in the former Soviet Union – to win a world title. And it came as late as 1975 in Vienna. This was itself extraordinary, given the fact that the Russians were always regarded as among the toughest of opponents, and that they generally figured in the medals of major events.

But the greatest accolade given to Nevzerov was that he beat the Japanese at their own game. For the speciality of this hard-training man was not in uranage or various sambo pick-ups, but in classical techniques – tai-otoshi, ippon-seoi-nage (left and right), osoto-gari, uchimata and ashiwaza.

It was an exceptional range for any fighter, but unheard of for a product of the Soviet Union. And winning the world -70kg title in 1975, and the Olympic title in Montreal the following year, proved that it was no fluke. He really was outstanding.

Nevzerov was born in Majkop, in the Northern Caucasus, and started sambo and judo at the major sports school there. The school was accustomed to producing champions – Nevzerov was followed there, a few years later, by Khazret Tletseri, who went on to win the world championships in 1983, and was three times European Champion.

The distinguishing feature of Nevzerov's character was that he decided success was the outcome of hard training. He was an inspiration for Alexander Iatskevich, who arrived at national training camps as a youth when Nevzerov was at his peak.

'I always remember seeing Nevzerov in training camps,' remembered Iatskevich in his book Russian Judo. 'Not only was he particularly gifted, but he also trained harder than anyone else.'

After the formal sessions, he would always stay on the mat, learning new moves, or go to the gym, for extra work. He was quite encouraging to the young fighters coming through, but concentrated mainly on his own practice.

1977. Nevzerov grips up with Neil Adams (Great Britain).

Nevzerov's main domestic rival was Valery Dvoinikov, a different kind of fighter who mixed sambo moves with classical judo. But Nevzerov beat him in the European final of the -70kg category in Lyons, and went on to beat him again in the world championships in Vienna.

His greatest moment was the Olympic Games in Montreal. No one was quite sure what kind of force he would be as he had missed the European championships that year. But the Japanese didn't have a force to match him. He went through his first three fights with ippons, his smooth, flexible style allowing him to shrug off coarse attempts to control him. Talaj (Poland), Hagmann (Switzerland) and Van Hoek (Netherlands) all succumbed.

In the semi-final, even South Korea's competent Chang-Sun Lee couldn't hold him, and was bowled over with left tai-otoshi for ippon.

The final pitted him against Koji Kuramoto (Japan) who, by calling on all his own classical judo background, was able to prevent ippon. It was kenka-yotsu, with Nevzerov's left stance against Kuramoto's right. But with the Russian's sparkling judo and perfect balance (and his professional tailored jacket) the result was never in doubt. He scored a koka from ippon-seoi-nage, another from tai-otoshi, and immediately afterwards, taking the sleeve and collar on Kuramoto's left, darted in for another tai-otoshi, scoring waza-ari. Kuramoto could answer only with a koka from a shoulder-throw – and the Soviet Union took their first Olympic gold medal in judo.

Nevzerov continued for another year. He won the European championships in Ludwigshafen in 1977, so that he could say that he held all the principal titles – Olympic, world and European – and then he retired. Such was the supreme determination and confidence of the man.

He taught at his old sports school in Majkop, becoming director there. He was retained, for a short while, as judo coach and teacher at the Racing Club de France in Paris, one of the main French judo clubs. But he was innately Russian, and not one of those who felt able to make his living abroad, however attractive the circumstances.

This was underlined by his personality – he was a private, self-contained man, who did not easily open up to others.

He became the Russian coach for the judo team at the Sydney 2000 Olympic Games, but left afterwards, and took a job in social work, caring for the deaf and mute. He remains a judo hero in his home country.

ANGELO PARISI

DOB **3 January 1953**
TOWN/COUNTRY **Arpino, Italy**
WEIGHT **-93kg/+95kg**
HEIGHT **1.85m 6ft 1ins**
OCCUPATION **Judo teacher and businessman dealing in martial arts equipment**

1977. Parisi throws Chochosvilli (Soviet Union) for Ippon with osoto-gari.

BEST RESULTS

Olympic Games
Munich 1972 bronze (Open) – for Britain
Moscow 1980 gold (+95kg) silver (Open) – for France
Los Angeles 1984 silver (+95kg)

European Championships
Ludwigshafen 1977 gold (Open) – for Britain
Paris 1982 gold (+95kg) – for France
Liège 1983 gold (+95kg)

French National Championships
gold five times

British Open Championships
1971 gold (-93kg)

FAVOURITE TECHNIQUES
Morote-seoi-nage (left and right), osoto-gari, ashiwaza

BORN IN Italy, but winning international medals for both Britain and France, Angelo Parisi has truly had an international career. During the 1970s and 1980s, until his retirement after winning a silver medal at the Los Angeles Olympics, Parisi was one of the most charismatic fighters on the circuit – or to be more precise, could be.

The manner in which he won his gold medal in the Moscow Olympics will never be forgotten – it was an astounding display of throwing skills by a heavyweight against, generally, much heavier opponents. Parisi could throw with equal facility to the left and right – holding both collars; and his opponents never knew which way he would spin. He could also throw comfortably forward with seoi-nage or backwards with osoto-gari. And his relaxed fighting method, which involved walking around the mat until he felt the opportunity was there, unnerved many a more stolid heavyweight.

In Moscow he had a bye in the first round, and then threw Wojciech Reszko (Poland). In the third round, it was the turn of Vladimir Kocman (Czechoslovakia). Paul Radburn (Britain) was next. In the final, he faced the defensive, yet awkward Dimitar Zaprianov (Bulgaria), but was determined, from the start, to end it well. This he did, after six minutes, with a remarkable left seoi-otoshi. He managed to get low under Zaprianov, and threw him high and hard with a perfect shoulder-throw.

This virtuosic throwing ability was Parisi's forte, and the talent showed itself early. His parents emigrated to Britain in the 1950s and started an ice-cream firm, making Italian ices. Parisi started judo in the London Schools Judo Association, and at the age of 15 joined The Budokwai, the oldest club in Europe and the home of many British champions. There he learned the smooth movement of his throwing skills, greatly improved by Brian Jacks, and he quickly rose to the top, winning European titles at espoir and junior level.

1983. Parisi throws Jehle (Switzerland) for Ippon with his tokui-waza, seoi-otoshi.

He represented Britain in Europe and then in the 1972 Olympics, aged only 19, he took a bronze in the Open. He subsequently married a Frenchwoman and emigrated to France. He was forced to miss the 1976 Montreal Olympics (the Olympic rule for change of nationality) but was at his peak as a heavyweight for Moscow four years later.

Angelo Parisi had a truly Latin temperament, which made him a very popular figure in France. He could be brilliant and he could be mediocre. He never really featured in the world championships – he failed to take a world medal of any colour. But under the Olympic flag, he came alive. In Los Angeles, he once again showed his talent by taking a silver – losing only to Hitoshi Saito on a penalty.

Parisi was once asked what was the secret of his judo. He replied: 'It is simple - I get my opponent on one foot and then I throw him.'

ROBERT VAN DER WALLE

DOB **20 May 1954**

COUNTRY **Belgium**

WEIGHT **-95kg, Open**

HEIGHT **1.89m 6ft 2.5ins**

OCCUPATION **Director of his own management motivational company**

BEST RESULTS

Olympic Games
Moscow 1980 gold (-95kg)/silver (Open)
Seoul 1988 bronze

World Championships
Paris 1979 silver (-95kg)
Maastricht 1981 silver (-95kg)/bronze (Open)
Moscow 1983 bronze (-95kg)/bronze (Open)
Seoul 1985 bronze (-95kg)
Belgrade 1989 bronze (-95kg)

European Championships
Ludwigshafen 1977 silver (-95kg)/bronze (Open)
Helsinki 1978 silver (-95kg)/bronze (Open)
Brussels 1979 silver (-95kg)/bronze (Open)
Vienna 1980 bronze (-95kg)/gold (Open)
Debrecen 1981 bronze (-95kg)
Paris 1983 bronze (-95kg)/silver (Open)
Liege 1984 silver (-95kg)/bronze (Open)
Hamar 1985 gold (-95kg)
Belgrade 1986 gold (-95kg)
Paris 1987 bronze (-95kg)
Pamplona 1988 bronze (-95kg)

FAVOURITE TECHNIQUES
Morote-gari, tsuri-goshi, harai-goshi, sukui-nage, osaekomi

PRINCIPAL PUBLICATIONS
Pick-Ups (Ippon Books)

Harai-goshi ippon on Szepsi (Hungary). Olympic Games, 1980.

ROBERT VAN DER WALLE, the Belgian champion, became something of a legend in his lifetime. His remarkable senior competitive career spanned nearly 20 years. Everyone facing him in the light heavyweight division knew that it was a fight to the finish. And when van der Walle had done the job there, he simply put on a fresh judogi and went into the Open competition, causing mayhem in much the same way. Some great judo champions are, at their hearts, judoka. Some are sportsmen. But Robert van der Walle was a fighter.

He fought in five Olympics, and virtually every world and European championships during that period. He won the Olympic -95kg title in 1980, the European Open title in 1984, and the European -95kg title in 1985. In 1989, at the age of 35, he was still up with best, winning a bronze (beating a young Stephane Traineau of France) in the world championships in Belgrade.

Van der Walle trained unremittingly. He was widely respected in Japan because of his tempestuous fighting style. He said once: 'I always was a strong fighter. When I took grip, my opponent generally knew about it.'

Yet although he was principally known for his morote-gari, his powerful two-leg pick-up which he did on most opponents from the beginning to the end of his career, he was also a surprisingly technical fighter. 'When I went to throw, I tried to use timing and the breaking of balance – both classical judo devices.'

When van der Walle was 19, and silver medallist at the world junior championships, he entered the European championships in London in 1974, and surprised everyone by beating Jean-Luc Rougé, the current title holder in the first round. Van der Walle admits it was just a fight – with merely five years of junior judo behind him, all he could do was grab legs, grab arms, attack with this, with that, and generally stun the Frenchman into bewilderment. Van der Walle went out the next round, but a valuable lesson was learned.

Six years later, at the Moscow Olympics, van der Walle was in his prime. He had trained in Japan, had won European bronze and silver medals, and had refined the raw morote-gari into a much deadlier weapon. He knew more precisely what to do with it – against left-handers, for example, he developed a sweeping style, levelling his opponents sideways. But he also used his hip throws – tsuri-goshi and harai-goshi and sukui-nage.

But he had never beaten Tengiz Khouboulouri, the great Soviet champion. In the months before Moscow, he worked with a friend in the judo club in Namur, studying videos of Khouboulouri and their fights, looking for a weakness. The answer, they felt, was sukui-nage. Van der Walle did thousands of uchikomi against the Khouboulouri grip – he even got friends to come up in the street and try to catch him unawares with a Soviet surprise. And in the final in Moscow, when Khouboulouri got his grip and attacked with his osoto-gari, van der Walle picked him up with sukui-nage and added the extra sweep to nail the throw. 'It looked like ippon, it felt like ippon, but only waza-ari was given,' recalls van der Walle. Twenty seconds later, the same pattern of attacks was repeated – this time producing the winning koka (van der Walle was given keikoku for stepping out, but the match was won).

Van der Walle had to dig deep in other ways as his career progressed. Four years later, at the Los Angeles Olympics, as strong as ever and very much the favourite, he was thrown in the first round by the American Leo White with makikomi. He was out of the event. His determined character would not allow him to disappear, and in Seoul in 1988, he was back again, and though 34 years old, still a huge threat. He seemed to be on course for gold again – until he was caught with a clean footsweep by the German Marc Meiling. Van der Walle returned in the repechage to win a bronze, giving the world a lesson in character and pride and sheer damn grit.

His success in his own category of light heavyweight overshadowed the fact that he was the last of the great open-weight category fighters (it is now the preserve of the heavyweights). He was often in the medals in the European Open event. But some of the great battles were behind closed doors – on the mat at Tokai University, van der Walle and Yamashita, good friends but fierce rivals, fought each other to a standstill during the traditional three-hour training sessions.

Van der Walle's tokui-waza, morote-gari.

Olympic final 1980. Van de Walle v Khouboulouri (Soviet Union). Khouboulouri attacks with osoto-gari and van der Walle counters for waza-ari.

NICOLAI SOLODUCHIN

DOB **3 January 1955**
TOWN/COUNTRY **Kursk, Soviet Union (Russia)**
WEIGHT **-65kg**
HEIGHT **1.64m 5ft 5ins**
OCCUPATION **Judo coach**

BEST RESULTS

Olympic Games
Moscow 1980 gold

World Championships
Paris 1979 gold
Moscow gold 1983

European Championships
Brussels 1979 gold
Helsinki 1978 silver
Paris 1983 bronze

BEST TECHNIQUES
Seoi-nage (standing and from the knees), uchimata, shimewaza (from standing), osaekomi, especially yoko-shiho-gatame

NICOLAI SOLODUCHIN was a stalwart member of the Soviet Union lightweight squad for over five years – a long time in a period when new faces seemed to appear all the time. An uncompromising fighter who was prepared to take hold of a fight and dominate by hard attacks, he was technically sound.

He first made an international impression at the European championships in Helsinki in 1978, losing only to the strong East German Torsten Reissman. But the following year, in typical fashion, he got to the final again, and this time made no mistake, beating James Rohleder (Germany). He went on to win the first of two world titles, holding Yves Delvingt (France), and making himself favourite for the Olympic title in Moscow in 1980.

This was the year of the boycott, which meant the absence of the Japanese team, and Soloduchin cruised to a gold. He caught Hector Rodriguez (Cuba) in a strong yoko-shiho-gatame, and used the same technique on his old rival, Torsten Reissman (East Germany). In the final, the Mongolian Tsendying Damdin managed to avoid being pinned, but lost on a shido – and knew he had been in quite a battle by the end.

Attacking Tsendying Damdin (Mongolia) in the 1980 Olympic Final, Moscow.

Soloduchin had only one more thing to prove to himself – that he could beat the Japanese. Absent through injury in 1981 when Kashiwazaki won the title, he put himself on the line again in Moscow in 1983, and once again used his strong ground-work to reach the final, where Yoshiyuki Matsuoka had no answer to his controlled aggression.

Soloduchin developed his own unique method of working his way out from between the legs of his opponent into yoko-shiho-gatame – especially useful against Japanese competitors who like to do newaza off their back. It involves forcing the opponent into the splits and is still taught by former Soviet Union coaches like Alexander Iatskevich today.

After his retirement, Soloduchin – always known for being a very open personality, helpful to all – returned to his home club as a coach.

1983. Extricating the leg and pinning Rosati (Italy) with his tokui-waza, yoko-shiho-gatame.

YASUHIRO YAMASHITA

DOB **1 June 1957**
TOWN/COUNTRY **Kumamoto City, Kyushu, Japan**
WEIGHT **+95kg/Open; actual weight: 127kg**
HEIGHT **1.80m 5ft 11ins**
OCCUPATION **Manager of the Japanese judo team 1989-2000. Now chief coach, Tokai University, and national educational adviser**

BEST RESULTS

Olympic Games
Los Angeles gold (Open)

World Championships
Paris 1979 gold (+95kg)
Maastricht 1981 gold/(+95kg) gold (Open)
Moscow 1983 gold (+95kg)

All-Japan Championships
1977-1985, gold

FAVOURITE TECHNIQUES
Osoto-gari, uchimata, ouchi-gari, yoko-shiho-gatame, okuri-eri-jime

PUBLICATIONS
The Fighting Spirit of Judo (Ippon Books)
Osoto-Gari (Ippon Books)

YASUHIRO YAMASHITA is Japan's most successful competitor, with an unbroken record of 203 wins. At 5ft 11ins and 127 kilos, he was not particularly tall for a heavyweight, and was frequently dwarfed by larger Europeans and Japanese. But his clear technical control and natural physical balance were allied to a remarkably determined spirit. Friendly and helpful in the dojo, even when a competitor, he was a different personality in competition – and sometimes in randori. He smiled a lot, but he once said: 'If people could tell from my face what was in my heart when I did judo, no one would practise with me.'

Yamashita began judo at the age of 9, and his talent was spotted early. In fact, he went to live with his grandfather in Kumamoto City on the island of Kyushu where he led his school team to national honours. In 1973 he won the national high-school tournament for the first time, and went on to join Tokai University, a key decision. Here, he trained under Nobuyuki Sato, who was to become one of the most successful of Japanese team managers.

In 1977, he won the All-Japan Championships for the first time. In 1978, when still only 19, Yamashita lost for the last time (in his whole

Pinning Grigori Veritchev (Soviet Union) to win the 1981 world heavyweight title.

competitive career, he only lost 16 matches) – against Yoshioka on a split decision at the national championships. He recalls determining afterwards to 'concentrate on giving all during the match,' and never relying on a decision. This deep-rooted will to win resulted in 203 consecutive victories until his retirement in 1985.

By 1979 Yamashita had already started to make an impact on international judo, surprising everyone by winning the Tournoi de Paris while still a teenager, and following up with the world heavyweight title in Paris in 1979. But he broke his leg in the final of the All-Japan weight category championships in 1980, against Sumio Endo (the match was recorded as a draw) and was not so affected by the Japanese boycott of the Moscow Olympics.

Three months after the accident, he was back in training. In 1981, at the world championships in Maastricht, Holland, he won both the heavyweight category and the Open, and the way he did so demonstrated that he was equally capable in standing and ground-work. Though his favourite technique was osoto-gari, he found it increasingly difficult to throw larger European opponents with it – especially as they knew his attacking movements. But his combination of ouchi-gari and uchimata, and his ashiwaza generally, combined with his mastery of gripping, gave him dominance in tachi-waza , and he was rarely seen to be under pressure. And his newaza – especially a combination of okuri-eri-jime and yoko-shiho-gatame – was equally commanding.

In the world championships in Moscow in 1983, he won the heavyweight category again. While he was continuing to win abroad relatively easily, at home all eyes were on another strong heavyweight talent, Hitoshi Saito, who was emerging to challenge Yamashita's control. In Moscow, Saito was given the Open category to defend – which he did successfully. Yamashita acknowledges that having Saito as a serious rival helped him continue through to the Los Angeles Olympics in 1984 on top form.

Yamashita fought only in the Open event in Los Angeles. His victory was regarded as a foregone conclusion – and he didn't seem to suffer from the pressure. But in the second round, against Arthur Schnabel (Germany), he pulled a muscle badly in his right leg, and limped out against Laurent Del Colombo (France). Colombo attacked with ouch-gari, and Yamashita, overestimating his own mobility, was stumbled, conceding a koka. It was the first time a non-Japanese fighter had ever scored on him.

'Suddenly, I heard an inner voice saying "What's wrong with you? Did you come to the Olympics to hurt your leg and lose the match?" When I heard that inner voice, I was back to being the strong Yamashita.'

He got up with his face set grimly, and shortly after, Colombo was thrown with ouchi-gari for wazai-ari, and held with yoko-shiho-gatame.

In the final, he crushed Mohammed Rashwan (Egypt), countering and clamping on yoko-shiho-gatame to win the gold medal. Yamashita remembers: 'The referee's call of ippon seemed to come from far away.

Throwing Gislason (Iceland) for ippon with his tokui-waza, left uchimata. Maastricht 1981 World Championships.

I stood in the middle of the loud cheers and I felt I was the happiest man in the world. I threw myself at Mr Sato, just like when I became Japanese champion at 19.'

Yamashita continued competing for one more year – winning the All-Japan Championships for a record ninth consecutive time, and then retired. He was 28. After the Seoul Olympics, he became manager of the Japanese team, and saw it through Atlanta and then Sydney, with some excellent results. He helped guide the Japanese team to new training methods, incorporating modern ideas while keeping traditional methods which he felt were valuable. But always he had a further goal.

Yamashita has always viewed judo in particular, and sport in general, as an important medium through which to develop individual personalities. A broadly educated, capable man, he was co-opted by the Japanese prime minister on a select committee to develop long-range planning for changes in Japanese education. After Sydney, he resigned as team manager, choosing to concentrate on teaching judo at Tokai University, and spending more time in education, both within sports and also with the disabled, in whom he has a particular interest.

Married with two children, he remains one of the most well-known and respected figures in Japan.

In The Fighting Spirit of Judo, his autobiography, and an account of his whole view of judo (Ippon Books 1993) he has written:

My record of 528 wins, 16 defeats and 15 draws, which surprises me even today, can be put down to the following factors:

1. I was never satisfied with my achievements, so I was striving for a better result all the time.
2. I was determined to realise my childhood dream to win the Olympic Games.
3. I was fortunate to have the right associates and circumstances.
4. I was very healthy and strong.

1979. Throwing Nowakowski (Poland) with left tai-otoshi.

ALEXANDER IATSKEVICH

DOB **25 March 1958**
TOWN/COUNTRY **Dobele, Latvia**
WEIGHT **-86kg**
HEIGHT **1.84m 6ft 0.5ins**
OCCUPATION **Manager, Belgium National Team**

BEST RESULTS

Olympic Games
Moscow 1980 bronze

European Championships
Helsinki 1978 gold
Vienna 1980 gold
Rostock 1982 gold

Tournoi de Paris
1978 gold

Tiblisi Tournament
1978, 1980, 1984 gold

World Junior Championships
Madrid 1976 gold

European Espoir Championships
Turku 1975 gold

FAVOURITE TECHNIQUES
Osoto-gari, tai-otoshi, ashiwaza, juji-gatame

PRINCIPAL PUBLICATIONS
Russian Judo (Ippon Books)

Iatskevich throws Peter Seisenbacher (Austria) with osoto-gari to win the 1980 European Championships.

ALEXANDER IATSKEVICH rose to the top of an indisputably tough tree – the Soviet Union. He had a steady growth, winning the European Espoir Championships in 1975, then the world junior title in 1976, and was ready to attack the senior ranks in 1978. He made a remarkable entry, winning the Tournoi de Paris in that year, when he threw the Japanese champion Seiki Nose several times in the final before armlocking him. In May of the same year, he beat Detlef Ultsch of East Germany to take the first of three European titles.

A mixture of disappointments and injuries saw him miss out on world medals, and only take a bronze in the Moscow Olympics. But he never lost his love of judo and he always maintained his keen interest in its techniques.

On his retirement, after winning his third European title in 1982, he began coaching in earnest, and in 1990 was invited by Jean-Marie Dedecker, manager of the Belgian National Team, to join him as coach. It proved a remarkably fruitful partnership, with Belgium producing a string of Olympic, world and European medals in the following decade.

Learning French and Flemish (adding to his English and German) in order to communicate directly with his players, Iatskevich had also the ideal background, with his knowledge of Russian-style judo combining with classical Japanese judo, to prepare the Belgian team for the modern judo of the day.

'Both systems have much to learn from each other,' he says in his book, Russian Judo – the first full study of the subject.

He became manager of the Belgian national team in 2000, and by his inspired but well-prepared coaching methods, continued the exceptional success the small country has had in international judo. Also, he has taken a leading role in giving a voice to judo coaches on an international level. He was the natural choice of the European Judo Union as the coach for the EJU men's team when they won the Intercontinental 2001 Millennium Cup.

He remains a fit and combative participant on the judo mat.

The famous Iatskevitch juji-gatame in action versus Strom (Sweden).

NEIL ADAMS

DOB **29 September 1958**

TOWN/COUNTRY **Coventry, Great Britain**

WEIGHT **-71kg /-78kg**

HEIGHT **1.77m 5ft 10ins**

OCCUPATION **Judo and health club owner**

BEST RESULTS

Olympic Games
Moscow 1980 silver (-71kg)
Los Angeles 1984 silver (-78kg)

World Championships
Paris 1979 bronze (-71kg)
Maastricht 1981 gold (-78kg)
Moscow 1983 silver (-78kg)
Seoul 1985 bronze (-78kg)

European Championships
Ludwigshafen 1977 bronze (-71kg)
Helsinki 1978 bronze (-71kg)
Brussels 1979 gold (-71kg)
Vienna 1980 gold (-78kg)
Rostock 1982 bronze (-78kg)
Paris 1983 gold (-78kg)
Liege 1984 gold (-78kg)
Hamar 1985 gold (-78kg)

Junior World Championships
Madrid 1976 bronze (-71kg)

Junior European Championships
Berlin 1977 gold (-71kg)

British Open Championships
Gold: 1977 and 1979-1985

FAVOURITE TECHNIQUES
Right tai-otoshi, right uchimata, yoko-tomoe-nage, juji-gatame, sangaku-jime

PUBLICATIONS and VIDEOS
A life in Judo, Armlocks (Ippon Books), Grips (Ippon Books), Tai-otoshi (Ippon Books), Ippon! (Fighting Films), Modern Competitive Judo (Fighting Films), The BJA Junior Syllabus (Fighting Films)

NEIL ADAMS is one of the best judo players from the west. Five times European champion, world champion in 1981, and twice Olympic silver medallist, he is one of a rare breed, a fighter with a European newaza style and a Japanese tachi-waza style. He has remained one of the best-known fighters in the world through his authorship of many books and as Fighting Films commentator.

On Adams' 7th birthday his father Cyril bought him a judo suit and took him to the local martial arts centre, a little wooden hut in a car-park in Rugby, for his first taste of judo. A year later, when his family moved, he transferred to Coventry Judo Club, his father acting as his coach. At first, his sole technique was morote-seoi-nage, but after suffering a serious injury executing the throw, he began developing right tai-otoshi. The wide split version was to become his tokui-waza.

In 1974, aged 16, he moved to London to train at the Budokwai – which was then in its heyday – alongside fighters like Olympic medallists Dave Starbrook, Keith Remfry and Brian Jacks. The charismatic Jacks inspired Adams – from Jacks he learned his spinning uchimata. He became European junior champion in 1977 defeating Ezio Gamba of Italy, by koka from tai-otoshi. Gamba was to be one of his principal rivals throughout his judo career. In the final of the British Open next year, Adams experienced a humiliating defeat that changed his whole career. The Frenchman Jean-Pierre Gilbert took him to the ground and strangled him with sangaku-jime. Forced to re-examine his ability on the ground, he worked hard on developing an unstoppable newaza attack. Remembering the skilful Russian Alexander Iatskevitch's victory over Toda (Japan) in the 1976 world junior championships, Adams chose the armlock, juji-gatame. For two years he honed his own unique version of the roll into juji-gatame into a world-class technique.

Adams says of himself: 'I was a skills parasite. Whenever I saw an exciting new technique I would pinch it, work on it for months and turn it into my own. I was hungry for as much knowledge as I could get.'

He began to take major scalps in senior competition. Throwing the Japanese champion Takahiro Nishida for ippon with uchimata in front of the Japanese crowd at the Kano Cup in 1978 remains one of his most memorable victories. In 1979 he beat Gamba (Italy) again, to win his first European title, but at the end of the year in the semi-final of the world championships in Paris, the Italian turned the tables, scoring yuko with left morote-seoi-nage, and Adams settled for the bronze. The next year at the Moscow Olympic Games they were to meet again, in the -71kg final, with the Italian winning by hantei, the narrowest of margins.

Following his loss in Moscow, Adams made the move up to the -78kg category. At the 1981 Maastricht world championships he produced a phenomenal range of techniques in the best performance of his life. He armlocked Olympic bronze medallist Ravdan Davadaali (Mongolia) with his newly perfected juji-gatame in the first round, threw Baptiste (Brazil) with uchimata in the second, and destroyed Latreche (Algeria) with two beautifully timed throws: an ouchi-gari for waza-ari and osoto-gari for ippon. A kouchi-gari for waza-ari on Kevin Doherty (Canada) took him into the final against the Japanese champion Jiro Kase.

Here Adams produced one of the most famous armlocks in the history of the sport, rolling Kase three times before straightening the arm to take the world middleweight title away from the Japanese for the first time.

Two years later, at the Moscow world championships, Adams was to lose his title, on a debatable split decision, to another Japanese, Nobutoshi Hikage. Convinced that he had done enough to win, it was the most disappointing loss he had suffered. But even greater disappointment was to follow at the 1984 Olympic Games in Los Angeles. Having stylishly thrown and armlocked his way into the final, he faced the unknown German, Frank Weineke. With the fight clearly under his control, he underestimated Weineke, and for the first and only time in a contest he was thrown for ippon, with a right uchimata/left ippon-seoi-nage combination. It was the lowest point in his career.

In 1985 he went hunting for Weineke, beating him in the final of the German Open. He went on to take his fifth European title, defeating the Russian Vladimir Chestakov in the semi-final, and the Pole Waldemar Legien in the final, throwing him for yuko with tai-otoshi. At the Seoul world championships he was disappointingly drawn against Hikage in the first round. The fight that should have been the final was decided by a chui penalty against Adams for stepping out. Hikage went on to win and Adams went through the repecharge to take the bronze, defeating Vismara (Italy), Doherty (Canada) and Legien (Poland) en route.

Neil Adams' contest career ended at the 1988 Seoul Olympics. He established his own health and judo club and became head coach to the British team for several years, during which time they had their most successful European Championship results. He is the author of a number of judo books, including *Armlocks*, *Grips*, and *Tai-otoshi* in the Ippon Books Masterclass series, and he is the familiar voice on all Fighting Films judo productions.

When asked the reason for his success, Adams says: 'Of course I had some natural ability, but more important than that was my belief that I would win. I made myself train harder than anyone else, so I knew I was better. Now, when I am coaching, I can see who is a potential champion: he is on time, trains harder, doesn't complain, and knows he is going to win.'

1983 British Open Final. Neil Adams throws Cerna (Mexico) for ippon with a totally committed right uchimata.

World Championships Final, Paris 1982. Versus Kruger (West Germany).

BRIGITTE DEYDIER

DOB **25 November 1958**
TOWN/COUNTRY **Montaubon, France**
WEIGHT **-61kg/-66kg**
HEIGHT **1.70m 5ft 7ins**
OCCUPATION **Director of Communications for La Poste Vice President, Federation Française de Judo**

BEST RESULTS

Olympic Games
Seoul 1988 silver

World Championships
Paris 1982 gold
Vienna 1984 gold
Maastricht 1986 gold
Essen 1987 silver

European Championships
Kerkrade 1979 gold (-61kg)
Undine 1980 silver (-61kg)
Pirmasen 1984 gold (-66kg)
Landskrona 1985 gold
London 1986 gold
Pamplona 1988 bronze

Fukuoka Cup
1986 silver
1987 bronze

FAVOURITE TECHNIQUES
Uchimata, kouchi-gari, juji-gatame

BRIGITTE DEYDIER was the dominant figure in the women's middleweight category for the major part of the 1980s, without obviously demonstrating the usual features of a champion. She was more careful and prepared than flamboyant, more tactical and technical than aggressive.

Deydier started judo at 14 in the small town of Montaubon because 'my brother and all my friends did judo.' Her first success came when she won the French championships in 1979, and she went on to win the Europeans in the same year – at -61kg. 'The French team was so strong at the time that if you won the national championships it meant you had a good chance to win the European championships', she said.

She trained hard and regularly, but it was only when she went up a category to -66kg (after recovering from a serious knee injury) that, with her physical and mental stability, she was able to prove herself a real international force.

In 1982, in Vienna, Deydier won her first world title with her uchimata much in evidence. 'At first, I could use uchimata directly, but later, as my opponents got to know it, I had to add combinations – kouchi-gari or tani-otoshi.' Few women were uchimata specialists at this time, and Deydier was also one of the few who regularly scored with juji-gatame.

In 1984 she won her second world title. The final match, against Irene de Kok of the Netherlands, she regards as one of her best. 'I think we were the best two in the category and so the final was at a high level, both mentally and physically. But we were very different in character – she was very agressive and I was more tactical, building up attacks.' At the end, Deydier was ahead only by a yuko from an uchimata/kouchi-gari combination achieved in the first minute, but it was extremely satisfying nevertheless.

A strong ude-gatame attack at the 1984 World Championships, Vienna.

The most disappointing moment in her career was in the final of the Olympic Games in Seoul when, looking in control of the fight against Sasaki (Japan), Deydier injured her knee and had to retire.

Though a busy professional in public relations, Deydier still practises from time to time. 'I always carry my judogi in my car, so that when I have a chance I can get on the mat,' she said. Characteristically, her interest is more centred on technique than on the ebb and flow of randori. 'I still enjoy working on technique,' she said.

EZIO GAMBA'S story is an extraordinary tale of an individual's triumph over politics in sport. Born in Brescia, in Northern Italy, he started judo aged nine when one of his friends used ashiwaza to knock him over in a fight. Mario Bernadini was the junior coach at his club, Forza e Costanza, who guided him up until the age of 13 when Franco Capelletti took over. Under Capelletti he became a spirited young fighter and an Espoir international, taking the silver to Chris Bowles (Great Britain) in the European Espoir Championships.

At 15 he moved to the College of the Italian Judo Federation and, under the guidance of National coach Matzushita Masami, added solid technique to his fighting spirit in twice daily judo sessions. His left dropping morote-seoinage and his left uchimata became world class techniques, and he became a formidable newaza exponent. In 1976, aged 17 he fought in the world junior championships in Madrid, losing in the final to Takahiro Nishida of Japan. The bronze medallist was Britain's Neil Adams. The three of them were to become rivals for the whole of their careers. The next year it was Adams who defeated Gamba in the final of the European junior championships.

In 1978 he enrolled in the Italian army and won his first major title at the world military championships. By 1979 he was representing Italy in the majors, but it was Adams who beat him in the final of the European Championships in Brussels. He knew he had to break the pattern of losses against the British fighter: 'He had excellent technique in both standing and ground work, and I spent many hours analysing his right handed fighting pattern. Before I went to sleep every night I lay in bed visualising how my left handed throws would beat him.' At the Paris world championships later that year they met in the semi-final. Gamba caught Adams cold near the beginning of the match, tucking under him with left seoi-nage for the decisive yuko. In the final he lost to Kyoito Katsuki (Japan), whilst Adams took the bronze.

As the 1980 Moscow Olympics approached it became evident that many governments might boycott the event in protest at the Russian invasion of Afghanistan, amongst them Italy. Gamba realised that, as the Italian judo team was enlisted in the military, there was a realistic possibility that they would be unable to compete so, six months before the Games, he started the process of extricating himself from the army. When Italy announced that those in the military would not be competing the Italian judo federation ceased training towards Moscow. So Gamba established his own training camp. He gathered together eight friends, all talented fighters: four local, two from Modena, 100 miles away, and two from Trieste, 250 miles away, as sparring partners. For two months they lived together, in Gamba's house, training with one aim, to win Ezio his Olympic gold.

When he was released from the army, (the only Italian athlete to be allowed to leave – all the others across many sports had applied too late), the Italian Federation realised that he would be fighting in Moscow and offered assistance. He was able to say: 'No thank you, my preparation is in hand!' He remembers: 'It was not ideal but with us living and training together, our spirit and my morale was very high.'

He travelled to Moscow a lone judoka whose desire to compete had overcome international politics. With the Japanese and South

EZIO GAMBA

DOB **2 December 1958**
TOWN/COUNTRY **Brescia, Italy**
WEIGHT **-71kg**
HEIGHT **1.77m 5ft 10ins**
OCCUPATION **National Coach of Italy**

BEST RESULTS:

Olympic Games
Moscow 1980 gold
Los Angeles 1984 silver

World Championships
Paris 1979 silver
Moscow 1983 silver

European Championships
Brussels 1979 silver
Rostock 1982 gold
Paris 1983 silver
Belgrade 1986 bronze

World Military Championships
1978 gold

Junior World Championships
Madrid 1976 silver

Junior European Championships
Berlin 1977 silver
Miskolc 1978 silver

FAVOURITE TECHNIQUES
Left drop morote-seoi-nage, left uchimata, right yoko-tomoe-nage, juji-gatame

Koreans absent, Gamba and Adams were favourites for the -71kg title. Gamba defeated Al Faran (Kuwait), Christian Dyot (France), B. Kim (North Korea) and Ravdan Davaadali (Mongolia) en route to the final where he met Adams. It was very close, seven minutes of attack and counter attack without score, and by decision Ezio Gamba became Olympic Champion.

But he knew his gold medal was tainted by the boycott and was determined to prove himself in the Los Angeles Olympics. At the Moscow world championships the year before he again took a silver, losing out to Japan's Hidetoshi Nakanishi. He knew that with Adams having moved up to -78kg his fiercest opponents in Los Angeles would be either Nakanishi or Byung Keun Ahn, the South Korean. In the the final he faced Ahn, who had defeated Nakanishi in the quarter final. Here he was caught with his own technique, a left seoinage for koka and had to settle for the silver. Bitterly disappointed, he felt he still had to prove himself the best.

His opportunity came shortly after the Games when he was invited to compete for Europe in the star studded continental team event in France. He won all his fights including the crucial tournament winning fight against Ahn in the Asia vs. Europe match, and he was awarded the trophy for European fighter of the tournament. For Gamba this was his greatest moment: 'In Moscow I beat everyone except the Asians, in Los Angeles I beat everyone except Ahn, in France I beat Ahn. I had proved myself the best in the world.'

After retiring from competition Capelletti persuaded him to coach at his club, from which he progressed to coaching the National Italian Team. Together with Felice Mariani he was responsible for guiding Maddaloni to his Olympic gold medal in Sydney. His love of judo still shines through in everything he does: 'I enjoy finding companionship with both my opponents and pupils. In Italy most of our athletes come from poor families and they learn that a strong heart and great energy can come from judo.' In coaching he is still very ambitious: 'I think with modern training and coaching methods it is easier to produce winners now than it was in my era. At the next Olympics we will do even better.'

When asked what were the special factors that made him a champion he replies: 'I accepted that it was possible to lose and be badly injured, and in accepting this I was prepared to risk everything to win. I had tunnel vision and would not allow anything else to distract me, but above all I loved what I was doing. I still do.'

1986 European Championships, Belgrade. A kouchi-gari into uchimata combination for ippon on Wieslaw Blach (Poland).

SHOTA KHABARELLI

DOB **26 December 1958**
TOWN/COUNTRY **Tblissi, Georgia**
WEIGHT **-78kg**
HEIGHT **1.78m 5ft 10ins**
OCCUPATION **National coach of Georgia**

BEST RESULTS

Olympic Games
Moscow 1980 gold

World Championships
Moscow 1983 silver

European Championships
Brussels 1979 silver
Debrecen 1981 bronze
Rostock 1982 silver
Paris 1983 bronze

FAVOURITE TECHNIQUES
'Khabarelli', ouchi-gari, pick-ups, leg-grabs

SHOTA KHABARELLI has had the distinction of having a technique named after him by the International Judo Federation (though curiously, he was not the first person to develop the technique – it was actually quite a common technique in the Georgian wrestling form of Chidaoba). The throw that came to be known as the 'Khabarelli' is a form of a pick-up using the trouser leg and (often) the belt, and is a most dramatic score when it comes off. It looks as if it requires a huge effort of strength, but it can be done in a highly technical and efficient manner.

In fact, the 'Khabarelli' was seen in judo before he used it so effectively in the late 1970s and early 1980s. It had been executed in international competition by other Georgians, especially by Chochosvilli in the 1970s. But Khabarelli could bring it off in a truly spectacular manner – and it worked because it came out of his all-action style, which saw him throw an arm in here, and a leg there, and grab what else he could as he wound his way in under his opponent's guard. From the 'Khabarelli' grip, he could also switch to ouchi-gari and other throws.

Khabarelli was in his prime at the same time as Neil Adams, and while he consistently beat the British technician, he regularly lost to lesser figures. He also had difficulty in domestic events. Curiously, though he won an Olympic title and brought back many medals at world and European level, he never won a national title in the Soviet Union. He was just known to present great difficulties for foreigners – and was selected on that basis.

His greatest moment was at the Moscow Olympics, where his non-stop attacking confused and then overwhelmed all opponents. Even such an experienced campaigner as Harald Heinke (East Germany) couldn't contain the irrepressible Georgian, who won on a koka. Neither could Mircea Fratica (Romania), another technician, who lost on a yuko; and a similar fate awaited Jose Ferrer (Cuba) in the final.

The amazing Khabarelli technique in action.

In the 1990s, the IJF decided to keep the names of all the official techniques in Japanese, and changed the pick-up 'Khabarelli' to hikkomi-gaeshi.

At the break up of the Soviet Union Khabarelli took over as national coach of Georgia. It was an extremely volatile time in many ways, yet Georgia has always been proud of its judo skills. Under the guidance of Khabarelli, the country managed to produce formidable teams and spectacular and original fighters, among them Georgi Vazagashvilli, George Revazishvilli and Nestor Khergiani.

In addition to producing unpredictable and determined fighters, Khabarelli added an extra element of strategy, using the weight categories to full advantage. Vazagashvili fought and won Olympic, world and European championships at -60kg, -65kg, -66kg, -71kg and -73kg; Revazishvilli was world silver medalist in 1997 at -60kg, and bronze medallist in 1999 at -73kg! The opposition are always kept guessing as to which Georgian will be fighting in their weight.

Shota Khabarelli today remains one of the most respected coaches in international judo.

SHINJI HOSOKAWA

DOB **2 January 1960**
TOWN/COUNTRY **Japan**
WEIGHT **-60kg**
HEIGHT **1.57m 5ft 2ins**
OCCUPATION **Judo coach**

BEST RESULTS

Olympic Games
Los Angeles 1984 gold
Seoul 1988 bronze

World Championships
Seoul 1985 gold
Essen 1987 silver

Kano Cup
1982 gold

FAVOURITE TECHNIQUES
Seoi-nage, tomoe-nage, ashiwaza, osaekomi

DURING SHINJI Hosokawa's term of ascendance he fought in the lightest weight but was one of the largest personalities in international judo. Whenever he fought, his supreme personal confidence lit up the mat, as he attacked ceaselessly, looking for the ippon that would finish the match. He was known to Japanese judo as 'the little giant.'

The final of the Olympic Games in Los Angeles was a typical Hosokawa moment. The Korean community had come out in force with sufficient flags in support of Jae-Yup Kim to match the Japanese support.

Hosokawa had dispatched Joao Neves (Portugal) with koshi-waza, followed by tomoe-nage for ippon; Luiz Shinoara (Brazil) lasted longer, but fell to seoi-nage and then another fast tomoe-nage for a second waza-ari; a yuko win over Felice Mariani (Italy) – tomoe-nage again – put him into the semi-final against Neil Eckersley (Britain). Eckersley's prowess at juji-gatame was nullified by a quick de-ashi-barai straight into yoko-shiho-gatame.

And then it was Jae-Yup Kim in the high-profile final. It turned out to be one of the shortest Olympic finals on record: Hosokawa took Kim to the ground, clamped on yoko-shiho-gatame and that was that.

It was a highly impressive major international debut and was to set the scene for further Hosokawa performances over the next Olympiad. The following year, Hosokawa – who trained at Tenri University – took the world title at Seoul, beating Peter Jupke (Germany) in the final.

In the world championships in Essen, Hosokawa lost to Jae-Yup Kim (Korea) at the end of a very fast uchimata right at the start of the contest – the fight was over in 27 seconds. Typically, in his preparation for the Olympic Games in Seoul in 1988, Hosokawa made a special study of uchimata-sukashi, and made good use of it in various contests. But he never got to use it against Kim to gain his revenge – for he lost, controversially, to Kevin Asano (USA) in the fifth round, and had to settle for the bronze. He was aghast.

After his retirement, Hosokawa went to teach in France, learning French. But he was also rapidly incorporated into the Japanese national coaching squad and was a prominent member of the coaching teams touring for subsequent Olympiads.

Uchimata sukashi ippon on Bartolomeu Dias (Angola). Seoul Olympic Games, 1988.

PETER SEISENBACHER

DOB **5 March 1960**
TOWN/COUNTRY **Vienna, Austria**
WEIGHT **-86kg**
HEIGHT **1.86m 6ft 1ins**
OCCUPATION **Judo teacher and coach**

BEST RESULTS

Olympic Games
Los Angeles 1984 gold
Seoul 1988 gold

World Championships
Seoul 1985 gold

European Championships
Vienna 1980 silver
Paris 1983 silver
Liege 1984 bronze
Hamar 1985 bronze
Belgrade 1986 gold
Paris 1987 bronze
Pamplona 1988 bronze

FAVOURITE TECHNIQUES
Osoto-gari, ouchi-gari, harai-goshi, maki-komi, juji-gatame

PRINCIPAL PUBLICATIONS
Modern Judo (Crowood)

1986. Attacking Miyoshi (Japan).

PETER SEISENBACHER won his first major international medal at the age of 20 – a silver at the European championships on home ground in Vienna in 1980, losing only to Alexander Iatskevich of the Soviet Union. Eight years later, perhaps to the surprise of many, he concluded a remarkable career by winning his second consecutive Olympic title – the first man ever to achieve this in the same weight category since judo was first seen at the Olympics in 1964.

During that time his judo, as he is the first to admit, changed drastically – though not the spirit behind that brave first silver. 'I went to Japan for the first time just after winning that silver in Vienna, and I thought I was quite strong. I was truly shocked by how many strong training partners were available in Japan – every other person I practised with seemed to me to be capable of winning a medal in a European championship!'

It was during this time that he began to introduce major changes. This was principally based on the way he practised. 'My judo was based on tension and condition. In dojos in Austria or elsewhere in Europe, I could keep it up for an hour or an hour-and-a-half, but against good opposition in Japan, for two hours or more, this was impossible.' He learned to fight less at close range, creating a distance between himself and his opponent – he now calls it a 'classical' distance. He broadened his range of techniques, also.

He was young enough to change, but not old enough to maintain winning form at the top level. It was three years before he won another European medal – a second silver in 1983. But already he had his eyes set on the Olympic Games in Los Angeles in 1984.

Seisenbacher formed a close bond with the Austrian national coach George Kerr, from Scotland, and the association was to play a key role in the two Olympic titles that followed. 'I wanted to be an Olympic champion to the exclusion of everyone and anything else,' admitted Seisenbacher, and in 1984 he was ready. 'My aim was to finish every fight as quickly as possible, especially the earlier ones, and so save energy for the later, harder bouts. He did exactly this, going through the first two rounds in less than two minutes, and was therefore still fresh when he faced Seki Nose (Japan) who had beaten him in the world championships the previous year. Luck went Seisenbacher's way when matte was not called during a manoeuvre from ground-work through standing and back to ground-work, and Nose relaxed, allowing Seisenbacher to catch him in a hold from which there was no escape. Throwing Fabien Canu (France) in the semi-final, he spoiled American hopes by throwing Robert Berland with tai-otoshi for ippon in the final.

He was the first Austrian gold medallist at the summer Olympic Games for 26 years, and became a national hero overnight. 'I was not prepared for the fruits of success,' he acknowledged, and needed quickly to cultivate the social skills necessary to match the attention.

It was two years before he was back in champion form. In 1986, in the European championships in Belgrade, he won the European title, beating Ben Spijkers (Holland). He even entered the Open, and threw Britain's heavyweight, Elvis Gordon, for ippon with kouchi-gari, before being thrown by East Germany's Henry Stohr.

And though he fared poorly in many competitions that followed, he once again had his sights focussed on the Olympics, this time in Seoul. 'Many people thought I was over the hill,' he said. Ten weeks before Seoul, Vladimir Chestakov of the Soviet Union beat him in the Hungarian Cup. 'But George Kerr told me that Mohammed Ali had always said that ten weeks is the maximum it takes to get ready for a fight, and this helped me to peak psychologically as well as physically at the right time.

The first two opponents were despatched for ippon. The third round, against Canu again, went the full time, but Seisenbacher won with tai-otoshi for yuko. Akinobu Osaka (Japan) was thrown with osoto-gari for yuko. He saw Frank Wieneke of Germany being thrown by Waldemar Legien with seoi-nage 13 seconds before the end, when it looked as if he was going to become the first man to win two consecutive Olympic judo titles. Was fate against this ambition for him, too?

No. In the final, Seisenbacher again met Vladimir Chestakov, but he was confident, while the Russian was playing safe. In the closing minute Seisenbacher upped the pressure, nearly scored with osoto-gari, and took the decision.

Looking back on his fighting career, Seisenbacher remarked: 'My second Olympic gold was the most satisfying for me. In Los Angeles I was 24 years old, I was a surprise winner – I surprised myself. I did not realise I could do it – it just happened. The second time I knew exactly what I was up against. I was older, and my personal circumstances had changed – I was married with a child, I was a celebrity in Austria, and the pressures from the outside were much greater.'

World Championships Final, Seoul 1985. Left osoto-gari ippon to defeat Georgi Petrov (Bulgaria).

MICHAEL SWAIN

DOB **21 December 1960**
TOWN/COUNTRY **Cranford, USA**
WEIGHT **-71kg**
OCCUPATION **Promotion and business**

BEST RESULTS

Olympic Games
Seoul 1988 bronze

World Championships
Seoul 1985 silver
Essen 1987 gold
Belgrade 1989 silver

Pan American Games
Caracas 1983 bronze
Indianapolis 1986 gold

Jigoro Kano Cup
1986 silver

Goodwill Games
Seattle 1990 silver

FAVOURITE TECHNIQUES
Tai-otoshi, ouchi-gari, kouchi-gari, juji-gatame

PUBLICATIONS and VIDEOS
Ashiwaza II (Ippon)
Mike Swain: Grappling (Century)
Mike Swain: Judo (Century)

Mike Swain looks on as Ahn (Korea) offers a prayer for his victory in the 1985 World Championships.

THERE IS a long tradition of judo in the USA and Americans have always provided strong competition in main international events ever since Jim Bregman won a bronze in the Tokyo Olympics.

But Michael Swain was the first American man to win a world title, when he beat Marc Alexandre of France to take gold in the world championships in Essen, Germany, in 1987. It was an exceptional achievement, for the lightweight category at the time was one of the strongest, and he had to overcome one champion after another. In the quarter-final, he met Toshihiko Koga, one of the most naturally talented and innovative fighters of his day. On their previous meetings, Koga had demolished Swain with his remarkable ippon-seoi-nage.

It was a tribute to the American that he never doubted his ability to win – even against Koga. In Essen, Koga launched him into the air for what looked like an inevitable ippon, but Swain managed to twist out. He recovered his mental composure superbly to produce a lightning-fast ouchi-gari, that sent Koga backwards for a koka – the winning score in a dramatic match.

Swain continued to fight on top form to contain Chang-Su Lee of North Korea in the semi-final, and then sweep past Alexandre in the final. With a silver medal in the world championships in Seoul in 1985, a second silver in 1989 (when he did lose to Koga) and a bronze in the Olympic Games in Seoul in 1988, Swain was clearly one of the most talented fighters of his era.

This was due, in large part, to his versatility. Swain started judo at the age of 11. An early hero of his was Allen Coage, Olympic bronze medallist in 1976, whose favourite techniques were tai-otoshi and ouchi-gari. These became the tokui-waza of Swain also.

Swain first went to Japan when he was just 17, demonstrating his love of judo and his courage! He arrived on his own, started at the Kodokan, and eventually joined Nihon University. 'It was like a boot camp,' he remembers, ' but I was on a mission, so I persisted.'

Through the long sessions at Nichidai (Nihon), Swain developed his style, building on the classical training he had received in America. Later, training in Europe and elsewhere, he learned to mix and match with the more physical Europeans – and it was this ability to cope with all styles that made him into such an effective fighting force.

He was USA national champion four times in his long fighting career, and won many other medals on the international circuit. He represented the USA at four Olympics, from 1980 to 1992.

Following his retirement, he turned to business, involving himself in martial art sales and competition promotion.

World Championships, Seoul 1985. Mike Swain counters Dyot (France) with sasae-tsuri-komi-ashi.

HITOSHI SAITO

DOB **2 January 1961**

COUNTRY **Japan**

WEIGHT **+95k/Open; actual weight: 140kg**

HEIGHT **1.80m 5ft 11ins**

OCCUPATION **National heavyweight coach and university judo coach**

BEST RESULTS

Olympic Games
Los Angeles 1984 gold (+95kg)
Seoul 1988 gold (+95kg)

World Championships
Moscow 1983 gold (Open)
Seoul 1985 silver (+93kg)

Asian Games
Seoul 1986 gold

Asian Championships
Jakarta 1981 gold
Kuwait 1984 gold

All-Japan Championships
1987 gold (Open)

Kano Cup
1982 silver (Open)
1986 gold (Open)

BEST TECHNIQUES
Uchimata, osoto-gari, kouchi-makikomi, tai-otoshi, ippon-seoi-nage, yoko-shiho-gatame, hara-gatame

EVEN THOUGH he was the first Japanese fighter to win two Olympic gold medals, for much of his prime time as competitor Hitoshi Saito had the misfortune to walk in the shadow of the great Yasuhiro Yamashita. Were it not for this, his list of gold medals would be much longer, for he was a formidable competitor.

At 140k, he was large – but he was flexible and highly technical too. One of his greatest assets was his fine sense of balance, which, allied with a surprising speed, made him always dangerous.

He first appeared in the West in 1983 at the age of 22, in the world championships in Moscow, taking some of the heat off Yamashita by being Japan's representative in the Open category. He never looked in the least flustered as he carved through the field, holding down Angelo Parisi (France) on his way to the final, where he comfortably beat Vladimir Kocman (Soviet Union).

He continued to appear as solid and unbeatable as a rock the following year, in the Los Angeles Olympics. A distinctively well-filled figure, with his huge, round and expressive face, Saito was a man to watch. Facing Cameroon's Silas, Saito complained about the tight sleeves of the jacket. The referee, perhaps persuaded by the size of Saito and the forcefulness of his protest, sent Silas off to have it checked. There was a delay.

Silas reappeared wearing the same jacket – the officials said it met the limits. Saito shrugged, wiped his big hand across his face, took hold of Silas and threw him immediately with uchimata for ippon.

In the next round, Kovacevic of Yugoslavia was thrown for ippon with uchimata, and the question was whether Angelo Parisi would go the same way in the final.

1988 Seoul Olympic rostrum.
Gold: Hitoshi Saito (Japan)
Silver: Henry Stoehr (East Germany)
Bronze: C. Yong Chul (South Korea)
Bronze: Grigori Veritchev (Soviet Union).

In the end, Saito had to rely on a shido given against the Frenchman, but the contest was technical and tactical, with both trying to break balance in classical manner.

How different was the final in Seoul the following year, when Saito expected to retain his title. He didn't count for a sudden death move from Jong-Chul Cho (South Korea) who took his one and only chance. As Saito, a left-hander, stretched his left arm forward to take hold of his opponent's lapel, Cho caught the arm and spun into waki-gatame. He took Saito to the ground and the armlock was on hard. Despite being in acute pain, Saito refused to submit, and eventually pulled his arm out without actually conceding a score. The Koreans in the stadium were going wild.

Saito complained that the move was illegal, and that Cho had tried to throw with an armlock. The referee and judges refused to accept the complaint, and forced Saito to continue fighting. He tried, but his left arm was seriously injured, and he couldn't take grip. He tried once more – but then conceded the fight.

He gained his revenge, and confirmed that he was an outstanding champion three years later at the Seoul Olympics, when he single-handedly upheld the honour of Japan. After six days of competition, with Yamashita having retired in 1985, Japan was without a gold medal – an unthinkable position.

It was left to Saito, and though he was clearly past his best, and his superb throws, particularly his uchimata, were no longer working, he saved the honour of the nation. He made the most of his excellent groundwork, taking one opponent after another to the ground and clamping on yoko-shiho-gatame, to win the gold.

Following his retirement, Saito, from Kokushikan University, was co-opted onto the Japanese national team as heavyweight coach.

CECILE NOWAK

DOB **22 April 1961**

TOWN/COUNTRY **St Amond les Eaux, France**

WEIGHT **-48kg / -52kg**

HEIGHT **1.62m 5ft 4ins**

OCCUPATION **French Senior Womens Coach**

BEST RESULTS

Olympic Games
Barcelona 1992 gold

World Championships
Belgrade 1989 bronze
Barcelona 1991 gold

European Championships
Helsinki 1989 gold
Frankfurt 1990 gold
Prague 1991 gold
Paris 1992 gold
Athens 1993 silver (-52kg)

TECHNIQUES
Left uchimata, left ogoshi, right sode-tsurikomi-goshi, utsuri-goshi, uranage

CECILE NOWAK started judo aged 11 at her local club, JCP Amondinois. Her coach, Monsieur Beaury remained her guiding force in the sport for 7 years. At 17 she won the Tournoi d'Orléans. It was her first big success and drew her to the attention of the selectors. She transferred to INSEP, the national training centre and met Guy Delvingt, the 1976 Junior European Champion, who coached her for the rest of her career: 'He was the best coach I have ever seen.' Delvingt recognised Nowak's mental strength and started to build her into a fighter who could take on the multiplc world champion from Great Britain, Karen Briggs.

Other fine French fighters, Marie Colignon, Fabienne Boffin and Martine Dupond prevented Nowak from making the European or world team, but eventually, in 1987, aged 26, she was selected for the world championships in Essen. The best moment in her career turned into the worst when she broke her knee during the competition. A massive operation was required and the full year of recuperation that followed would have finished most fighters. But in 1989 Nowak fought her way back into the team for the Europeans. She made it to the final where she met Briggs and, to everyone's surprise, beat her to take the title.

Later that year, in the world championships, she met Briggs again and was countered for ippon. Briggs went on to her fourth world title and Nowak took the bronze. In 1990 they fought twice: In the final of the Frankfurt European championships Nowak won and in the final of the European team event it was Briggs who took the honours. They knew each other inside out and expected to meet in every final. In the 1991 European final it was Nowak's turn again, but at the world championships in Barcelona another factor had to be taken into account – Ryoko Tamura. The Japanese fireball was nearly 15 years younger than Nowak and enormously talented. Nowak was drawn on one side with Briggs and Tamura on the other. The French champion defeated Jana Perlberg (Germany) with a stunning ippon ogoshi to reach the final. Once more, it was Briggs, who had defeated Tamura, that she had to face. It was the last and closest of all their fights. Nowak fought the more upright fight, looked more dominant, and took the world title by decision.

At the Barcelona Olympics Nowak was on sparkling form: after a first round bye she blitzed Hulya Senyurt (Turkey) with a massive right handed sode-tsurikomi-goshi, defeated Giovanna Tortora (Italy) in the quarter final and flattened Salima Souakri (Algeria) with a left handed uchimata for ippon in the semi-final. Having beaten Briggs, Tamura faced her in the final. Early in the fight Nowak scored koka with a two- handed leg grab. As the contest progressed Tamura started to open up. Just when it looked as if she might turn the tables Nowak countered her ashiwaza, catching her leg with one hand and bundling her over for another koka. The two scores were sufficient. Experience had triumphed over youth. It was the finest victory of her life.

Following the Olympics Nowak moved up to the -52kg category taking silver at the 1993 European championships. Soon after she retired and moved to coaching, becoming French senior women's coach in 2001.

When looking to produce champions she searches for someone like herself: 'First, they must have spirit and inner belief – I believed in myself totally. They must have a strong character be prepared to push themselves on their own, not just when the coach is there. They can be in excellent shape, but when they come up against another fighter with the same physical capacity it is mental strength that will win the day. Mental strength can overcome great technique.' Her ambition now is to make the French women's team the strongest in the world.

Konica

INGRID BERGHMANS

DOB **24 August 1961**
TOWN/COUNTRY **Luik, Belgium**
WEIGHT **-72kg/Open**
HEIGHT **1.80m 5ft 11ins**
OCCUPATION **Health and fitness clubs**

BEST RESULTS

Olympic Games
Seoul 1988 gold (-72kg)

World Championships
New York 1980 gold (Open)/bronze (+72kg)
Paris 1982 gold (Open)/silver (-72kg)
Vienna 1984 gold (Open)/gold (-72kg)
Maastricht 1986 gold (Open)/silver (-72kg)
Essen 1987 silver (Open)/silver (-72kg)
Belgrade 1989 gold (-72kg)

European Championships
Udine 1980 silver (Open)/silver (-72kg)
Madrid 1981 silver (Open)/bronze (-72kg)
Genoa 1983 gold (Open)/silver (-72kg)
Landskrona 1985 gold (-72kg)
Paris 1987 gold (Open)/silver (-72kg)
Pamplona 1988 gold (Open)/gold (-72kg)
Helsinki 1989 gold (-72kg)/bronze (Open)

Fukuoka Cup
1983 gold (Open).gold (-72kg)
1984 gold (Open); silver (-72kg)
1986 gold (-72kg); bronze (Open)
1987 gold (-72kg); bronze (Open)

FAVOURITE TECHNIQUES
Uchimata, osoto-gari, ouchi-gari, kouchi-gari, juji-gatame, osaekomi

IN THE early years of women's judo, the most prominent figure was the statuesque Belgian Ingrid Berghmans. She made an unforgettable impression partly because in most of the big events she fought twice – in her weight category and in the Open – and often won both. What's more, she achieved this in an elegant and decisive manner – her judo fighting style was upright and clean, and her intention was always to go for the big dramatic throw. 'Flop and drop' techniques were simply not in her repertoire. She liked nothing better than to up-end her opponent with a sweeping, classical-style uchimata.

This happened no more dramatically than in the final of the 1984 world championships in the -72kg category against Barbara Classens (Germany). Berghmans was a waza-ari down, when, with just a few seconds to go, she manoeuvred Classens to the edge of the mat and threw her with a superb uchimata to snatch the title.

But, above all, Berghmans will be remembered for the way she handled much bigger opponents in the Open category. This she did by a combination of spirit and determination – and sensible gripping and attacking.

A typical example was the final of the Open category at the world championships in Maastricht in 1986. She faced the giant Chinese Jin-lin Li, who was nearing two metres, and weighed 116 kilos, giving Berghmans a handicap of 44 kilos. But by maintaining perfect hit and run tactics, Berghmans dominated the fight and took the title – one of six world gold medals.

Part of her success was her confidence and ability in both tachi-waza and newaza. Her uchimata was her main threat (and she did it in text-book nage-no-kata style); she also used sukui-nage, and kouchi-gari – sometimes in combination with kuchiki-taoshi. Her main newaza threat was juji-gatame, which she learned from Neil Adams.

Her consistent medal-winning form made her a great star in her own country too – for a while, Robert van der Walle and Ingrid Berghmans were the country's most famous sports couple. She certainly inspired the next generation of women judo champions, in her own country, and elsewhere.

It was once written of her: 'Berghmans epitomizes the concept of the modern female athlete. She is strong, powerful, skilful, and yet beautiful and feminine.'

Ingrid Berghmans throws Barbara Classens (West Germany) for ippon in the semi-final of the 1987 European Championships.

FRANK WIENEKE

DOB **31 January 1962**
COUNTRY **Germany**
WEIGHT **-78kg**
OCCUPATION **German national coach**

European Championships, Belgrade 1986. Kosoto-gari ippon on Metsola (Finland).

BEST RESULTS

Olympic Games
Los Angeles 1984 gold
Seoul 1988 silver

European Championships
Belgrade 1986 gold
Pamplona 1988 silver
Helsinki 1989 silver

European Junior Championships
San Marino 1981 silver

BEST TECHNIQUES
Ippon-seoi-nage, uchimata, te-guruma, kosoto-gake, shime-waza. Kumi-kata in attack and defence

THE HEAD of the German judo delegation at the Los Angeles Olympics wanted to visit Disneyland, and asked his coach which was the day guaranteed not to produce a medal for Germany. The coach suggested he should go on the day of the -78kg category. Young Frank Wieneke was promising, explained the coach, but he was just out of the junior rankings and had some way to go.

The head of the German judo delegation went to Disneyland on the suggested day, and on that day Germany, through Wieneke, won its first Olympic gold medal in judo.

It was an astounding victory, for Wieneke had never won a medal in a major international event, apart from a silver at the European junior championships in San Marino in 1981. What's more, the -78kg category was, according to all pundits, the preserve of Britain's Neil Adams who had looked totally dominant all year.

Furthermore, Wieneke's draw was difficult. He started with the Japanese champion, Hiromitsu Takano, but Wieneke, totally unexpectedly, threw him with an uchimata/kosoto-gake combination. Then he threw Walid Mohammed (Egypt) with seoi-nage and won on a shido from Kevin Docherty (Canada). After a decision win over Mircea Fratica (Romania), Wieneke was in the final – and everyone thought he had won an unbelievable silver.

The previous year, at the European championships in Paris, Adams had met Wieneke and won on a small score. Curiously, the Briton had rolled Wieneke into juji-gatame position but couldn't finish it. The warning bells should have sounded then.

In Los Angeles, the final was going to form. Adams was finding it difficult to penetrate Wieneke's strong defence but was well ahead on attacks and looked secure. Suddenly, in the red area on the edge of the mat, Wieneke attacked with right uchimata drawing a strong left-arm push-away defence from Adams. Instinctively, doing a combination he had never consciously done before, Wieneke spun into a very fast drop left ippon-seoi-nage, spinning Adams over for ippon. It was the biggest upset of the judo tournament in the 1984 Games.

The great question was whether Adams had been caught by a lucky throw. The following year, Wieneke didn't figure in the European or world championships. In 1986, he fought very aggressively to win the European title in Belgrade, but in 1987 again failed to feature in the medals in the world championships.

He was keen to prove that Los Angeles had not been just a lucky break. And, by winning a silver in fine style in the Olympic Games in Seoul, he proved just that. Looking in prime condition, he strangled Peter Reiter (Austria), threw Lars Adolfsson (Sweden) with a hip throw for yuko and Spain's Victor Gonzalez for ippon with a fast uchimata. He edged past Pascal Tayot (France) on a koka, then overpowered Torsten Brechot (East Germany) to, yet again, reach the Olympic final.

There he met the one man who had consistently beaten him throughout his career – Poland's Waldemar Legien. Both attacked spiritedly, and with 16 seconds to go, it looked as if Wieneke would win a decision. But that was not the way Wieneke saw it. He thought he was behind and attacked. Legien avoided and taking his opportunity, threw with ippon-seoi-nage for ippon, a mirror image of how Wieneke himself won four years before.

Wieneke responded like a gentleman. He picked himself up and, after the bow, lifted Legien's arm in the air in acknowledgement of the superb concluding throw.

Afterwards, Wieneke said: 'My best tournament ever was Seoul. I was perfectly prepared, I was mentally strong, I showed my best judo. Everything I was able to do, I did in Seoul. It was important for me to reach the final after what some people called the lucky shot four years ago. It showed me I was a member of the top players.'

There was a strange pattern to Wieneke's career. He was strong on every even year – 1984, 1986, 1988 – but weak on uneven years. He was especially dangerous when he was in the red area of the mat. Many fine throws were produced there. And it was only after his Olympic gold medal that he practised the uchimata/ippon-seoi-nage combination – which he was to score with subsequently, even though everyone knew it.

Technically, his judo was varied and strong, with outstanding kumi-kata. As a person he was totally focussed on the mat – unforgiving in randori and competition. Off the mat, courtesy ruled.

After his retirement, he became a regional judo coach, and, in 2001, took the post of national coach and team manager. He has remained fit and strong and bang on his fighting weight. He is married with children, and has always kept pets – big dogs and reptiles (including snakes).

Olympic Final, Los Angeles 1984. Throwing Neil Adams (Great Britain) for ippon with uchimata into ippon seoi-nage combination.

KAREN BRIGGS

DOB **11 April 1963**
TOWN/COUNTRY **Hull, Great Britain**
WEIGHT **-48kg**
HEIGHT **1.50m 4ft 11ins**
OCCUPATION **Judo teacher and mother of two**

Briggs' tokui-waza, tomoe-nage in action at the Barcelona Olympics 1992.

BEST RESULTS

World Championships
Paris 1982 gold
Vienna 1984 gold
Maastricht 1986 gold
Belgrade 1989 gold
Barcelona 1991 silver

European Championships
Oslo 1982 gold
Genoa 1983 gold
Pirmasens 1984 gold
London 1986 gold
Paris 1987 gold
Helsinki 1989 silver
Frankfurt 1990 silver
Prague 1991 silver

Tournoi de Paris
1992 gold

Fukuoka Cup
1983, 1984, 1985, 1986, 1988 gold

British Open Championships
1981, 1982, 1983, 1987, 1989 gold

FAVOURITE TECHNIQUES
Tomoe-nage, ouchi-gari, tai-otoshi, ippon-seoi-nage, sangaku roll to kami-shiho-gatame

PUBLICATIONS and VIDEOS
Judo Champion (Crowood)
Modern Competitive Judo (with Neil Adams) (Fighting Films)

KAREN BRIGGS is widely regarded as the first woman champion to be a complete fighter. Many men, sceptical about women's competitive judo in the early 1980s, grudgingly acknowledged that she had all the attributes of a champion – clean and varied technique, perfect fitness, fierce fighting spirit, and a speed and determination that took her to the top.

In a long and distinguished career, she won four world titles, six European titles and numerous other events. Equally strong in groundwork as in standing, she appeared almost unbeatable from the time she won her first world title in 1982 in Paris, to her last world title in 1989 in Belgrade – apart from when injuries incurred in matches and training. She fractured her leg in two places going for her fourth successive world title in Essen in 1987 (though she tried to carry on fighting...). And she dislocated her shoulder holding down Fumiko Esaki (Japan) when regaining the title.

Karen Briggs' competitive career was coming to an end at the time that women's judo was accepted on the Olympic programme, and she retired after dislocating her shoulder again in the semi-final of the

Semi-Final Barcelona World Championships, 1991. Briggs brilliantly turns and pins Ryoko Tamura (Japan) for ippon with yoko-shiho-gatame.

Barcelona Olympics against Ryoko Tamura, the Japanese champion. Significantly, Tamura always stated that Karen Briggs was the fighter she most admired in judo.

Briggs was born in Hull, in the north of England, and was naturally talented at sport. She started judo at a small club, and when she first emerged on the national scene, beating world champion Jane Bridge, was known for terrier fighting tactics but little technique. It was a tribute to her tenacity and intelligence that, guided by Roy Inman, the outstanding British national women's coach, she pursued modern sports training methods to develop peak fitness, and a tightly constructed fighting pattern that demolished all comers.

She was best known for a very fast yoko-tomoe-nage, which often scored ippon. When it didn't she went straight into groundwork, generally using a sangaku turnover to move into kami-shiho-gatame. Her drop-down tai-otoshi and ouchi-gari were also major scorers for her.

Briggs was totally professional in her preparation. She instituted a punishing daily fitness regime, which involved running, swimming, weights and stretching. She realized early in her career that fitness had to be attained by careful planning and execution, and this paid huge dividends. In her early years of competition she was fairly stiff, but taught herself to stretch until she became usefully supple. Strength at extension was also important, and weight-training was a key element in developing this. All her fitness programmes were carefully planned to bring her to peak condition at the big events.

'Many people felt that it didn't matter whether they won or lost in randori or even competition, but I didn't think like that. I wanted to win. It meant everything to me – not to beat the other person but to set myself a personal challenge and meet it in the best possible way. I didn't like to think I was wasting my time.'

ca

ica
HOUS

WALDEMAR LEGIEN

DOB **28 August, 1963**
TOWN/COUNTRY **Byton, Poland**
WEIGHT **-78kg/-86kg**
HEIGHT **1.80m 5ft 11ins**
OCCUPATION **Judo coach at the Racing Club de Paris**

BEST RESULTS

Olympic Games
Seoul 1988 gold (-78kg)
Barcelona 1992 gold (-86kg)

World Championships
Essen 1987 bronze (-86kg)
Belgrade 1989 bronze (-78kg)
Barcelona 1991 bronze (-86kg)

European Championships
Hamar 1985 silver (-78kg)
Belgrade 1986 bronze (-78kg)
Frankfut 1990 gold (-86kg)

FAVOURITE TECHNIQUES
Ippon-seoi-nage, kouchi-gari, waki-otoshi to the left, uchimata, ouchi-gari, kosoto-gari to the right

Final Barcelona Olympic Games, 1992. Throwing Pascal Tayot (France) with ko-soto-gari.

WALDEMAR LEGIEN is one of very few fighters who have won two Olympic gold medals. His success was at two different weight categories, yet it seemed that the change of weight didn't seem to have much relevance. When he won his first gold, in Seoul in 1988, he was a true -78kg fighter, coming down to make the weight. Four years later, in Barcelona, he had already acclimatised to the -86kg category, but he was the lightest of his weight class, tipping the scales at only 82kg. More than anything, it was his awareness of strategy and his fighting style – keeping opponents at a distance – that allowed him to overcome fighters who were physically much bigger and stronger. 'I was not very strong physically and I couldn't compete if I came in close. But I was very mobile: even when I was only 82k, and competing at -86kg, I could attack from a distance quickly.'

In the 1970s and 1980s, Poland did not have a large judo fraternity. Legien estimates that there were only 5,000 judokas in the country. The lack of numbers was compensated by an advanced understanding of sports science, and for the top fighters, regular training trips to Japan and Korea. Though formally from an 'eastern bloc' country, his judo was fairly traditional.

He started judo at 9, which was unusually young, because most started at 13. He was attracted to it because 'there was lots of movement and variety.' As he went through the junior ranks, his talent showed itself. Morote-seoi-nage and ouchi-gari were his strong techniques. As he grew taller for his weight, this changed to ippon-seoi-nage on the left, and morote-gari (he had seen the Belgian champion Robert van der Walle in a competition once, and admired his success with the leg-grab).

Sports training in Poland made much of sound physical preparation, good mental or psychological work, and imaging – visualising techniques in operation and combat situations. Legien also thought much about strategy

– when to attack, how to attack, when to rest, when to change pace,when to switch from defence to attack, when to feign injury, how to use the rules.

'We were taught very well in Poland,' recalls Legien. A key factor for him was 'to attack when your partner was not ready.' A particularly good time for Legien was when his opponent thought he was too tired to attack. A precise, fast attack would often bring the decisive score. One signficant occasion when this worked was in the final of the Olympic Games in Barcelona against Frank Wienecke (Germany) – an attack 11 seconds from the end ensured victory.

Not only did he change weight, he also changed his techniques as his career progressed. In the Olympic Games in Seoul, he threw almost exclusively to the left. In Barcelona, he went both left and right. And while he was competent on the ground – as a junior, he was very much a juji-gatame exponent – he relied on tachi-waza at senior level. A year after retiring, he joined the Racing Club of Paris, one of the leading French judo clubs, and was still technical director there eight years later. His intention is to produce good technical players.' I love good judo,' he said.

World Championships, Belgrade 1989. Throwing Austrian Peter Reiter with a drop seoi-nage for ippon.

DIANE BELL

DOB **11 October 1963**
TOWN/COUNTRY **Crawcrook, Britain**
WEIGHT **-56kg/-61kg**
HEIGHT **1.65m 5ft 5ins**
OCCUPATION **British national women's coach**

BEST RESULTS

Olympic Games
Barcelona 1988 gold (-61kg)

World Championships
Maastricht 1986 gold (-61kg)
Essen 1987 gold (-61kg)
Barcelona 1991 silver (-61kg)

European Championships
Pirmasens 1984 gold (-56kg)
Landskrona 1985 bronze (-56kg)
London 1986 gold (-61kg)
Paris 1987 bronze (-61kg)
Pamplona 1988 gold (-61kg)
Helsinki 1989 silver (-61kg)
Frankfurt 1990 silver (-61kg)
Athens 1993 bronze (-61kg)
Den Haag 1996 bronze (-61kg)

Fukuoka Cup
1985 bronze (-56kg)
1986 bronze (-61kg)
1987 bronze (-61kg)
1988 bronze (-61kg)

FAVOURITE TECHNIQUES
Morote-seoi-nage, okuri-eri-jime

IN THE mid 1980s, as women's judo consolidated its presence on the international competitive circuit, Diane Bell proved one of the most consistent fighters, demonstrating that a serious attitude toward training and preparation can result in top-class results. Her record of two world titles, Olympic gold (in Barcelona, when women's judo was a demonstration sport) and three European titles should be noted against a background of an exceptional steadiness: from 1984 to 1990 she won a medal of some kind every year in the European championships – seven in succession, at a time when European women in her weight category were generally the strongest in the world. And she came back to finish with another bronze in 1996.

Diane Bell started judo in Crawcrook Judo Club, a small town near Newcastle in the north-east of Britain. Despite its size, the club regularly provided leading members of the British women's team over a number of years.

Bell first represented Britain at -56kg, and was one of the tallest in her category. She had some international success, winning her first European title in Pirmasens in 1984 and a bronze a year later. But that year she decided to swap weight categories with Ann Hughes, who fought at -61kg. The decision was made after both returned from an international trip without a medal between them – Hughes was a few inches smaller than Bell, and so one took weight off while the other put it on.

The result was instantaneous. In Maastricht, 1986, they both won world titles within a few minutes of each other. Bell had to overcome two obstacles – in an early round she dislocated a finger, but knowing that if the doctor manipulated it she would be disqualified, she snapped the finger back in place herself, carried on fighting, and won. In the final, against Celine Geraud (France) she was slightly behind on attacks until the last two seconds. She launched a powerful and precise ouchi-gari, and scored as the bell went.

Her competition success then seemed to dim. She failed to win an event all year, taking only a bronze at the European championships, and wasn't a favourite to retain her world title in Essen in 1987. Surprisingly, she scythed through all her opponents, looking the champion from the moment she stepped on the mat. When asked afterwards how she managed such a transformation, she commented: 'I was concentrated all through the day.' It didn't matter who was the opponent, Bell knew she had a job to do, and did it. She went on to take the gold in the Seoul Olympics (with a superb uchimata sukashi against Noriko Mochida) therefore holding all three principal international titles at the same time.

She was never known as a fighter with spectacular techniques. She had a good drop morote-seoi-nage, and was particularly dangerous with a fast strangle in newaza.

1996. Strangling Sara Alvarez (Spain) with kata-ha-jime to take her last European medal.

But Bell's great asset was that she was extremely fit, tactically clear, difficult to throw and had good simple gripping skills. All her opponents knew that to face Bell meant, almost certainly, that the fight would go to full time, and that Bell would be as strong – if not getting stronger – in the last minute as in the first.

She benefitted from having Hughes as her training partner at events during her peak years, and the coaching skills of British women's team manager Roy Inman to add to her club coaches Wyn and Rob Bolton.

On retirement, she became senior women's coach of the British squad.

MIRIAM BLASCO

DOB **12 Dec 1963**
TOWN/COUNTRY **Vallodollid, Spain**
WEIGHT **-56kg**
HEIGHT **1.60m 5ft 3ins**
OCCUPATION **Judo coach and Senator to the Spanish Senate**

BEST RESULTS

Olympic Games
Barcelona 1992 gold

World Championships
Barcelona 1991 gold
Belgrade 1989 bronze

European Championships
Helsinki 1989 bronze
Prague 1991 gold
Paris 1992 bronze

Tournoi de Paris
1989 bronze
1991 silver
1992 gold

FAVOURITE TECHNIQUES
Osoto-gari, tai-otoshi, ouchi-gari, uchimata, juji-gatame, sangaku-jime

ON THE 31st July 1992, at 8.00 pm, in the packed Palau Blaugraña stadium in Barcelona, Miriam Blasco made history. She not only won the -56kg lightweight Olympic gold medal but more importantly became the first Spanish woman to win an Olympic gold at any sport. As a result she shot suddenly to national stardom and brought judo to a level of recognition in Spanish society that would have been previously unimaginable.

Miriam Blasco's career started 21 years before in a small judo club, El Gimnasio Kobiyashi, in Vallodollid. When she was eight her father, Angel, a keen sportsman himself, enrolled Miriam and her sister, Coqui, at the local judo club, which was run by a friend of the family, Alfonso Lago. Sport was already ingrained into family life. Nearly all Miriam's eight brothers and sisters were involved in one sport or another, Angel coached the local gymnastics team and Miriam's mother, Maria del Carmen, owned and ran a sports shop, 'Blasco Deportes.' As if they had an inkling of what the future might hold, the logo for the sports shop pictured a triumphant figure, hands aloft, holding up the Olympic rings!

As a junior Blasco was not an exceptional judoka. But at 18 she left Vallodollid to live in the coastal town Alicante, with her husband Alfredo, where she met the coach Sergio Cardell, who would shape her career and make her believe in the possibility of an Olympic gold medal. By 1984 she had taken several national medals. Cardell convinced her that, with harder training, she could win the national championships. Blasco responded but the result was three consecutive bronze medals. Aged 24 she agreed to give it one last shot, deciding that if she didn't win the 1988 national championships she would retire.

At last, she won the Spanish title. It was a crucial win in her career, one which remains among her most memorable. Quick to seize the moment, Cardell proposed a serious four-year plan towards the Barcelona Olympic Games. He introduced a gruelling fitness programme, and twice daily judo sessions. 'Sergio taught me how to compete and how to train, and he taught me my groundwork,' says Blasco. They studied technique using a video camera and used circuit drills to perfect Blasco's tai-otoshi, osoto-gari, ouchi-gari, uchimata, juji-gatame and sangaku-jime, techniques that were to become the trademark of the right handed fighter.

Just one year after she very nearly retired, Blasco took the silver at the 1989 European championships in Pamplona and then, later in the same year reached the semi-final of the Belgrade world championships against the fine French fighter Cathy Arnaud. With 30 seconds to go Blasco was leading by virtue of a yuko from osoto-gari but was buried with a massive right seoinage by the French fighter. However she won the bronze match to take her first medal at the world championships.

In 1991 she took her first European title, defeating Marsman (Netherlands) in the final and went to the world championships in Barcelona as one of the favourites. She scored ippon all the way through to the final, dispatching the talented Korean Sun-yong Chung in the semi-final with a beautiful uchimata in just 10 seconds! In the final she faced Nicole Flagothier of Belgium. When Flagothier attempted uranage Blasco countered her with ouchi-gari for a waza-ari which won her the title in front of her ecstatic home crowd and installed her as favourite for the Games.

However at the European Championships in 1992 she was defeated by decision in the semi-final against the British fighter Nicola Fairbrother. Though she took the bronze she knew that Fairbrother would be a significant force at the Games that she would have to deal with. As the Olympics approached tragedy struck. Just one month before the Games Sergio Cardell was killed in a motorbike accident. It was a devastating blow to Blasco but she determined to fight on and win the medal they had strived for together.

Blasco's draw gave her a bye in the first round and a re-match with the Korean Chung in the second. This time it was not so easy, and both fighters were wound up to keikoku, before Blasco caught her with ouchi-gari for ippon. Next was a knife edge match against Tateno (Japan) which Blasco scraped through on a split decision. In the semi final she armlocked the great Cuban fighter Driulis Gonzalez, to come up against Fairbrother (Great Britain) in the final. In front of a packed, 10,000 strong, fervent Spanish crowd, including the King and Queen, Blasco went a yuko ahead from a take back and managed to survive both a sumi-gaeshi koka and a powerful shimewaza attack by the Briton to take the Olympic title. In memory of her coach the crowd chanted 'Sergio, Sergio' as Blasco celebrated.

Blasco's reign at the top of the -56kg division was relatively short lived but during 1991 and 1992 she dominated the division. During those two years Blasco held the European, world and Olympic titles and won gold medals in Paris, Prague, Warsaw, Rome and Holland. Shortly before the 1996 Atlanta Olympic Games Blasco retired from international competition. She had been part-time coaching for the last 4 years and chose to turn full-time. Two of her pupils won Olympic bronze medals in Atlanta.

In 1996 Blasco opened her own judo club in Alicante, and she continues to change the face of Spanish sport. In 2000 she was elected by the public to be Senator for Spain's governing party, el Partido Popular. 'La Senadora Olimpica', as the newspapers have nicknamed her, is the first sportswoman to enter the Spanish Senate.

Ippon harai-maki-komi at the 1991 Barcelona World Championships.

AURELIO MIGUEL

DOB **10 March 1964**
COUNTRY **Brazil**
WEIGHT **-95kg**
HEIGHT **1.78m 5ft 10ins**

BEST RESULTS

Olympic Games
Seoul 1988 gold
Atlanta 1996 bronze

World Championships
Essen 1987 bronze WC
Hamilton 1993 silver
Paris 1997 silver

Tournoi de Paris
1988 silver

Junior World Championships
Mayaguez 1983 gold

FAVOURITE TECHNIQUES
Left tai-otoshi, left ouchi-gari, left drop seoi-nage, left uchimata

THE BRAZILIAN Aurelio Miguel is the best judo player to emerge from South America, with an extraordinary international career span of 15 years. But for two narrow defeats to the canny Pole, Pavel Nastula, he could have been a multiple world and Olympic champion.

His first success came in the 1983 world junior championships in Mayaguez, Puerto Rico, where he won his category, displaying the strong grips and tactical brilliance that became his trademark. Four years later, at Essen, he took his first senior world medal, a bronze. In 1988, Miguel shocked the judo world. At the Seoul Olympics, in the same category as Hitoshi Sugai (Japan) and Robert Van de Walle (Belgium) he emerged champion, incredibly without scoring a single koka! He fought five full-length contests, beating Stewart (Britain) and Fridriksson (Iceland) by decision, and Fazi (Italy), Sosna (Czechoslovakia) and finally Meiling (Germany), all by chui. In 25 minutes of judo he tactically outplayed and out gripped everyone to take the gold.

Four years later, at the Barcelona Olympics, he started identically, beating Mbomba (Zaire) by hansoku-make and Sosna by keikoku, but was thrown, first by the eventual winner, Antal Kovacs (Hungary) and then by the bronze medallist Dimitri Sergeev (Unified Team), both times with uchimata.

Tactically brilliant, Miguel was also a fine left-hander. In particular, his double step left tai-otoshi was world-class and, combined with a dancing ouchi-gari, could catch the best. At the 1993 world championships he ran Kai (Japan) up the penalties in the quarter-final and scraped a split decision against Sergeev (Russia) in the semi-finals. But in the final the Hungarian Olympic champion Antal Kovacs threw him for ippon with his running leg-grab.

Miguel emerged again at the 1996 Olympics fighting under the

Miguel's tokui-waza, left skip tai-otoshi against Papaioannou (Greece) in the open category of the 1997 Paris World Championships.

name of Fernandes. A beautiful left uchimata on the Mauritian Felicite helped him into the semi-final against the world champion Pavel Nastula of Poland. Nastula was a tactician, but the Brazilian still managed to wind him up to keikoku, and looked set for his second Olympic final. With 19 seconds to go Miguel attacked with a half-hearted ouchi-gari and Nastula piled him over with a kosoto-gari counter, to score a winning waza-ari. In the bronze fight against Sonnemans (Netherlands) Miguel produced a classic left skip tai-otoshi for the medal.

At the 1997 world championships the same throw worked to devastating effect on several occasions. In round two he threw Keith Davis (Great Britain) for ippon in the dying seconds of the match. Against Ghislain Lemaire (France) in the semi-final he threw him twice with the same technique, for waza-ari and ippon, to set up the final against Nastula, a very close affair between two left-handed tacticians. Nastula scored first, a drop seoi-nage for yuko. Miguel equalised with left ouchi-gari, which Nastula just avoided. Both wound the other up to keikoku and the decision was split in the Pole's favour.

But Miguel was not content and three days later added spice to the Open category. His draw gave him massive men, but he breezed through two rounds, throwing Papaioannou of Greece and the Latvian Darznieks for ippon in identical style, with the left tai-otoshi. The eventual winner, Rafael Kubacki (Poland), stopped him, with an ashiwaza ippon. After another victory in the repecharge he lost against another huge man, Dennis Van der Geest (Netherlands), who threw him with drop seoi-nage for ippon. However, for a -95kg fighter, 7th place in the open category was a fine achievement.

It is to be hoped that the exploits of the enduring Brazilian will inspire a new generation of even greater fighters to emerge from South America.

FENGLIAN GAO

DOB **15 October 1964**
COUNTRY **China**
WEIGHT **+ 72kg / Open**
HEIGHT **1.86m 6ft 1ins**

Maki-komi: world championships, Vienna 1984.

BEST RESULTS

Olympic Games
Seoul 1988 (demonstration event) silver

World Championships
Vienna 1984 silver (+72kg)
Vienna 1984 bronze (Open)
Maastricht 1986 gold (+72kg)
Essen 1987 gold (+72kg)
Essen 1987 gold (Open)
Belgrade 1989 gold (+72kg)

TECHNIQUES
Left maki-komi, left kosoto-gari, right maki-komi, kesa-gatame

FENGLIAN GAO was the first, and arguably the most successful, of a series of Chinese female heavyweight fighters, which included Jin-lin Li, Ying Zhang and Di Zhang. Indeed in the first three official women's Olympic judo tournaments the Chinese won the super heavyweight title with Xiaoyan Zhuang, in Barcelona 1992, Fuming Sun in Atlanta 1996 and Hua Yuan, in Sydney 2000. Four times world champion, Gao was an awesome presence on the mat, a giant of a woman, large boned and strong. She was easily the biggest competitor in the events she fought in.

Like many of the early female international heavyweights her major technique was a massive maki-komi (which she could do to both sides) into an unbreakable kesa-gatame. Once her weight was launched into the throw she was virtually unstoppable. Her first appearance on the international scene was at the 1984 Vienna World Championships, aged 19. This was the first time that Chinese women had taken part in IJF events. In the +72kg she was beaten in the final by Marie-Teresa Motta from Italy. In the Open she picked up the bronze behind Ingrid Berghmans (Belgium). But this was the last time she would lose in the world championships for the next six years.

Two years later in Maastricht she won her first world gold medal defeating Marjorie van Unen of the Netherlands in the final. Her team mate Jin-lin Li took the silver in the Open weight category. The following year the men's and women's world championships were combined for the first time in Essen, and the 22 year old Gao was at her peak.

She fought in both the +72kg and the Open and she was quite simply unbeatable. The +72kg category was the qualifying event for the 1988 Olympic demonstration event and Gao took the gold ahead of Regina Sigmund (West Germany), who took the silver, and Angelique Seriese (Netherlands) and Margie Castro (United States) who picked up the bronzes. In the Open she defeated Ingrid Berghmans in the final for her third world title.

World Championships Open Weight Final, Essen 1987. Versus Ingrid Berghmans (Belgium).

At the Olympic Games in Seoul Gao was the favourite for victory. She defeated Sigmund again in the semi-final and came up against Angelique Seriese in the final. Seriese outgripped her and ran her around the mat. Gao could not settle enough to launch her attacks. Seriese won by decision to take the gold, and it was the most disappointing moment in Gao's career.

But in 1989 the Chinawoman was back with a vengeance, at the Belgrade world championships. This time she was only contesting the +72kg. In the second round she threw and pinned Tzvetana Tomova (Bulgaria) with ushiro-kesagatame, in the quarter-final she defeated Sharon Lee (Great Britain) with a couple of kokas and in the semi-final she armrolled the enormous Russian Svetlana Gundarneko into first ushiro-kesagatame and then switched to yoko-shiho-gatame for ippon. The final against Regina Sigmund (West Germany) was a disappointment. Both fighters knew each other well and there was no score in a negative fight. Gao came close with a kosoto-gari attack and won by decision to take her fourth world title. It was the last time she would be seen on the international stage.

Other Chinese fighters continued to dominate the heavyweight women's category for many years, some with considerably more stylish judo, but Fenglian Gao was the first to show the world the massive potential of Chinese Judo.

World Championships, Maastricht 1986. Holding Paque (France).

KAORI YAMAGUCHI

DOB **28 December 1964**
TOWN/COUNTRY **Fukuoka, Japan**
WEIGHT **-52kg**
HEIGHT **1.60m 5ft 3ins**
OCCUPATION **National judo coach & judo teacher at Tsukuba University**

BEST RESULTS

World Championships
New York 1980 silver
Paris 1982 silver
Vienna 1984 gold
Maastricht 1986 silver
Essen 1987 silver

Asian Championships
Jakarta 1981 gold
Kuwait 1985 gold

Fukuoka Cup
1983 silver
1984 silver
1985 gold
1986 gold
1987 silver

National Japanese Weight Category Championships
10 times gold (consecutively)

FAVOURITE TECHNIQUES
Kouchi-gari, tai-otoshi

KAORI YAMAGUCHI was the first female Japanese player to command international respect. This was partly for her consistency. From the first world championships in New York in 1980 she appeared in every world final until her last silver in 1987, an extraordinary result even if, during that time, she won only one gold – in Vienna in 1984. Her commitment and her technique was admired by all.

Yamaguchi will be particularly remembered as an extremely stylish technician, at a time when the international standard of women's judo was maturing. Perhaps above all, she had an outstanding kouchi-gari. She threw most opponents at least once with it, setting them up with skilfull gripping and movement, before sweeping the leg away in classical style.

Her stance was upright and firm, her fitness never in doubt. Just how far ahead of her contemporaries she was in her home country could be seen by the fact that she won the All-Japan weight category championships ten times in a row – as well as two golds and three silvers in the Fukuoka Cup.

When she started judo as a child, at the age of six, there were very few girls in the dojo – and it was still relatively unusual for girls to practise with boys. Not for Yamaguchi, whose combative spirit and love of judo drove her to practise with everyone.

She explains how she came to favour kouchi-gari because she was always practising with boys or men who were more powerful than she was. 'I couldn't do throws where power was needed because I could not match their power,' she said. So she concentrated on throws which relied on timing – above all kouchi-gari.

It was a particularly appropriate choice for her international competitive life. 'I found that foreigners tended to go backwards after 'hajime'. And I could do kouchi-gari on people going backwards.'

Yamaguchi's intelligent attitude to judo continued after her retirement. She was immediately fast-tracked by the national organisation. She went to England for a year to study English, and, on her return, became closely involved with the women's national squad which was already beginning to produce some outstanding fighters.

It was her ability to absorb Western ideas without losing the classical Japanese approach to judo that has made her invaluable to women's judo in Japan. She also broadcasts for Japanese radio and television on judo.

Neat ashiwaza at the 1984 World Championships, Vienna.

JAE-YUP KIM

DOB **17 May 1965**
TOWN/COUNTRY **Daegu, Korea**
WEIGHT **-60kg**
HEIGHT **1.71m 5ft 7ins**
OCCUPATION **Entrepreneur**

Uchimata hane-goshi ippon on Mohammed Madhar (Surinam) at the Seoul Olympics, 1988.

BEST RESULTS

Olympic Games
Los Angeles 1984 silver
Seoul 1988 gold

World Championships
Essen 1987 gold

Asian Championships
Damascus 1988 bronze

Tournoi de Paris
1987 bronze

Junior World Championships
Mayaguez 1983 gold

Sungkop Tournament Seoul
1987 silver

FAVOURITE TECHNIQUES
Drop seoi-nage, kouchi-gari, uchimata, kani-basami

JAE-YUP KIM was Korea's most successful lightweight, arch-rival of the great Japanese competitor Shinji Hosokawa in the -60kg category. His favourite technique was drop seoi-nage, but he also had an excellent left uchimata, and a strong kouchi-gari. On the ground, he favoured shimewaza, and as a surprise would occasionally throw in a strong kani-basami, the flying scissors technique, subsequently banned by the IJF. In 1983, aged 18, he became world junior champion at Mayaguez, Puerto Rico, beating the Chinese fighter Zhu in the final. Over the years Kim's natural weight increased considerably, but he continued to diet down to 60kg.

In 1984, Kim was selected for the Los Angeles Olympics. With a bye in the first round, he beat Carlos Cotillo (Spain), Guy Delvingt (France) and Eddie Liddie of the USA to get into the final. Here he met Hosokawa for the first time and was quickly overwhelmed, pinned with yoko-shiho-gatame for ippon in one minute and nine seconds. Three years later, in Essen, he met Hosokawa again, in the final of the 1987 world championships. Hosokawa was fully expected to win, having added the world title in 1985 to his Olympic crown. But Kim had other ideas. He was now considerably stronger and, in a total reversal of their Olympic final, threw Hosokawa for ippon with uchimata-makikomi within seconds of the start. He was immediately established as favourite for the Olympics the following year, on his home ground in Seoul. But Kim was under severe pressure in Korea. As well as continuing weight problems, he had a serious domestic rival at -60kg, Hyun Yoon. At the Korean Olympic trials Yoon defeated Kim, and the selectors were left with a headache. Kim believed his chance of fighting in Seoul had gone and that Yoon would be selected.

Then, in a last minute decision, swayed by his great performance in the previous year's world championships, the Korean judo federation selected Kim for the -60kg. With only two weeks to go to the Games, Kim found himself weighing 69kg! In order to lose nine kilos he went on a spartan diet of plain boiled rice and raw fish slices – and made the weight in time for the start of the Games.

Olympic Final, Seoul 1988. Attacking Kevin Asano (USA).

As one of the sports at which the home nation was most likely to win medals, the judo was held in the huge Changchung stadium. The judo competition itself was truly spectacular, and unlike any seen before in the sport. Drums, flamboyant cheerleaders and a roar from the packed ranks of spectators greeted the arrival of any Korean fighter. Kim had five fights to reach the final, and defeated Mohamed Madher (Surinam), the unorthodox Georgian fighter, Amiran Totikashvili (Soviet Union), Pessoa of Brazil, Helmut Deitz of Germany and Patrick Roux (France) en route to the gold medal match. Here he fully expected to meet Hosokawa again, but the Japanese fighter was surprisingly beaten by Kevin Osano of the United States in the semi-final. The final was a tight affair, but with the excited crowd behind him Kim defeated the American by shido, and took the Olympic gold to rapturous applause. Afterwards he told the press that he believed the medal he had won also belonged to the man he had displaced for the Korean -60kg Olympic spot, Hyun Yoon.

After retirement from competition he went on to work as one of the coaches for the Korean national team, before establishing his own business.

UDO QUELLMALZ

DOB **8 March 1967**
TOWN/COUNTRY **Leipzig, Germany**
WEIGHT **-65kg**
HEIGHT **1.75m 5ft 10ins**
OCCUPATION **Performance Director, British Judo Association**

BEST RESULTS

Olympic Games
Barcelona 1992 bronze
Atlanta 1996 gold

World Championships
Belgrade 1989 silver
Barcelona 1991 gold
Hamilton 1993 bronze
Makuhari 1995 gold

European Championships
Pamplona 1988 bronze
Frankfurt 1990 silver
Athens 1993 bronze

Junior European Championships
Cadiz 1984 gold
Leonding 1986 bronze

German Championships
Gold: 1987, 1988, 1990, 1992, 1994, 1996 (-71kg)

FAVOURITE TECHNIQUES
Left tai-otoshi, left ouchi-gari, left kouchi-gari, left hiza-guruma, left de-ashi barai, left osoto-gari, okuri-eri-jime, hadaka-jime, kata-ha-jime

PRINCIPAL PUBLICATIONS AND VIDEOS
Olympic Judo Quellmalz (Fighting Films)

UDO QUELLMALZ is the most successful lightweight competitor produced by the West. Between 1989 and 1996 this left-handed German -65kg competitor returned from every world championships and Olympic Games with a medal, culminating in his victory in Atlanta, where his performance was the most dynamic of the 1996 Olympic judo tournament. He subsequently became the head of elite player coaching in Great Britain.

Even though his greatest successes came after the Berlin wall came down in 1989, Quellmalz is a product of the East German sports system. He started judo aged seven in Leipzig, East Germany. At 14 he was spotted by state scouts and enrolled in the Leipzig Children and Youth Sports School, attended by teenagers training in Olympic disciplines. Judokas trained alongside wrestlers, fencers and handball students. Morning academic work was followed by 4 hours of conditioning and technique training in the afternoon. Here he met the most influential coach of his career, Karl-Heinz Deblitz, who oversaw his judo until he left for the West.

Deblitz taught Quellmalz what he regards as a typically East German but very valuable lesson: that if the fight were to be stopped at any time you should be the winner. This meant having maximum fitness and never being behind on attacks or scores.

Aged 17, Quellmalz was selected for the Cadiz Junior European championships, an under 21 year-old event. He fought his way to the final and came up against Sergei Kosmynin of the Soviet Union. The fight remains his most memorable:

'It was a seven minute final. I made the mistake of scoring a yuko in the first 30 seconds. He came at me non-stop for six and a half minutes. I stayed ahead, but at the end I couldn't even hold my arms up. However, I knew then, having beaten many older fighters, I had the chance to be really good.'

At 19 he left school, an established East German senior national squad member. His greatest disappointment remains not being selected to compete in the 1987 Essen world championships in front of a German crowd. Despite having won a bronze medal in the Tiblisi Cup, one of the world's strongest tournaments, he was not regarded as ready for the world championships. But the next year his first senior European medal qualified him for the Seoul Olympic Games. He was thrown with tomoe-nage by world champion, Yamamoto of Japan, in the second round.

In 1989 everything changed for Quellmalz: he had a great world championships in Yugoslavia, only losing in the final to home favourite Dragomir Becanovic; the Berlin Wall came down; and he moved to the West, to Abensberg, in Bavaria. Later he switched to Ingolstadt, remaining there for the rest of his competitive career. He found that training was less rigorous than in the East, but because of the strength of his grounding, with now no risk of over-training, he still achieved great results. A quiet, self-motivated fighter, he developed a good relationship with national coach Dietmar Hoetger, and extended his range of techniques.

Quellmalz's continuous attacking style was backed up with a range of left-handed throws. His tokui-waza was left tai-otoshi, but it was his formidable ashi-waza, in particular kouchi-gari, that set things up and won him countless contests. Another great strength was his rapid transference to newaza, and the strangles okuri-eri-jime, kata-ha-jime and hadaka-jime.

Olympic Games, Atlanta 1996. The throw of the tournament: hiza-guruma ippon on Hernandez (Cuba).

World Masters, Munich 1996. Quellmalz's newaza favourite okuri-eri-jime.

His first world championships victory came in Barcelona in 1991, defeating Okuma of Japan in the final. At the Olympics the following year he came unstuck against the winner, Sampaio of Brazil, losing by chui, but took the bronze. At the European championships in 1993, he fought the Russian Sergei Kosmynin again, and was thrown for ippon with a massive hiza-guruma. Watching it on the video afterwards, Quellmalz was impressed by the beauty of the technique and determined to build it into his repertoire. That year he took a bronze in the world championships, losing to Switzerland's Eric Born by split decision, but throwing Jimmy Pedro of the USA for waza-ari with left osoto-gari. The winner was Japan's Yukimasa Nakamura, whom Quellmalz met in the 1995 world championships final in Japan. In the last seconds of the fight Nakamura launched a huge kosoto-gari attack, only to be landed flat on his back with Quellmalz's kouchi-gari counter.

Quellmalz's tokui-waza, left tai-otoshi, on Karazelid (Kazakhstan) at the 1993 World Championships. Scored ippon by referee Shozo Fujii.

In the Atlanta Games Quellmalz started as favourite, and had a fantastic day, producing a series of great ippons. In the second round he dispatched the dynamic Cuban, Hernandez, with the throw of the tournament, his recently acquired hiza-guruma. A perfect tai-otoshi on Belgium's Philip Laats put him into the final against Nakamura. The fight was very close, with a kouchi-gari kinsa swaying the split decision in Quellmalz's favour. He remembers his relief as he came off the mat: 'I threw my jacket away, and thought, that's it - holiday at last!'

He regards the reasons for his success as: 'having some natural talent with good co-ordination, having the right coaches at each different stage of his development, and having personal motivation and confidence on the mat. You can only get real confidence when you've done all the training and you've got some good results behind you. Then confidence in your own ability becomes the deciding factor.'

Quarter Final Olympic Games, Atlanta 1996. Tomoe-nage waza-ari on Almeida (Portugal).

TOSHIHIKO KOGA

DOB **21 November 1967**
TOWN/COUNTRY **Fukuoka-ken, Kyushu, Japan**
WEIGHT **-71kg ; -78kg**
HEIGHT **1.69m 5ft 7ins**
OCCUPATION **Appointed to coaching team, Japanese womens squad 2000**

BEST RESULTS

Olympic Games
Barcelona 1992 gold (-71kg)
Atlanta 1996 silver (-78kg)

World Championships
Essen 1987 bronze (-71kg)
Belgrade 1989 gold (-71kg)
Barcelona 1991 gold (-71kg)
Makuhari 1995 gold (-78kg)

Junior World Championships
Rome 1986 gold (-71kg)

All Japan Open weight Championships
1990 silver

Kano Cup
1986 gold

All-Japan weight Championships
1988 gold (-71kg)
1989 gold (-71kg)
1990 gold (-71kg)
1991 gold (-71kg)
1992 gold (-71kg)
1995 gold (-78kg)

FAVOURITE TECHNIQUES
Ippon-seoi-nage, seoi-nage, koshi-guruma, sode-tsuri-komi-goshi, kouchi-makikomi, tomoe-nage

PUBLICATIONS and VIDEOS
Koga – A New Wind (Fighting Films)

TOSHIHIKO KOGA is one of the most innovative and exciting fighters the sport has ever seen. What sets him apart from other competitors is the amazing range of throws he invented that have since become an accepted part of modern judo. Think of one-handed seoi-nage and somersaulting sode-tsuri-komi-goshi and you think of Koga. Whilst other great traditional Japanese fighters seemed predictable, if unstoppable, Koga was both unorthodox and brilliant.

As a six-year-old Toshihiko started judo training with his eight-year-old brother Motohiro under the guidance of their father Toshiro. The three of them would run together every morning, and after training each night at the local dojo Toshiro would take the boys through everything they had learned, repeating the lesson again at home. Motohiro ruled his younger brother with an iron will, often forcing him to do the chores – and even the homework – for both of them. Maybe because of this, by the time he was eight Toshihiko held a 5th dan in Shodo, the art of Chinese calligraphy, and was ultimately forced to choose between the tatami and the brush.

At the age of 11 the brothers moved to Tokyo to train at the Kodogakusha, a boarding school for promising judoka with a spartan regime, where Toshihiko trained under Kazuo Yoshimura, whom he still regards as one of the most influential coaches in his career.

However, it was his older brother who taught Koga his tokui-waza, standing ippon-seoi-nage. Motohiro was becoming a good competitor, winning junior tournaments with ippon-seoi, and Toshihiko longed for the same success. Motohiro was an exacting teacher and Toshihiko learned the technique quickly, partly because he did not want to be shouted at by his brother any longer! Motohiro progressed to become a fine international competitor, winning the 1985 Shoriki Cup at -71kg, but in the same year they came to a crossroads that was to change their lives. Both of the Koga brothers entered a major tournament, held at the Kodokan, and both made it to the final. Motohiro and Toshihiko describe the match as being like fighting themselves, so alike was their judo, but, unexpectedly, Toshihiko was to emerge the winner, armlocking his brother with juji-gatame. Immediately after this fight Toshihiko remembers Motohiro saying to him: 'Over to you, little brother', and he effectively then abandoned competitive judo to become a high school PE teacher back in Kyushu.

For Toshihiko, however, this was the turning point in his competitive career and, now out of his brother's shadow, he started to turn in great performances of his own. He obliterated everyone with ippon-seoi-nage to win the 1986 world junior championships, and threw Mike Swain of the USA with the same technique for ippon in the final of the Kano Cup the same year. But it was also at this time that he badly injured his right elbow, and this forced him to adapt and change his fighting style. In his video, *Koga – A New Wind* he explains: 'I worked to develop techniques in such a way that they didn't put stress on my elbow. Such techniques inevitably involved not using the conventional grips and approaches and throwing from unusual angles or throwing one-handed. I hoped that by doing techniques that my opponent did not expect I would be able to make up for the fact that I couldn't use my elbow in my judo.'

In 1987 Swain defeated him in the semi-final of the world

championships, scoring a koka with ouchi-gari. Swain became champion and Koga went on to take the bronze. But two years later, using all the unusual new techniques that have become his trademark, Koga became world champion at -71kg for the first time, throwing North Korean Chang-Su Lee with an incredible one-handed seoi-nage in the semi-final, and defeating Swain in the final.

World Championships, Belgrade 1989. The throw of the tournament. Chang-Su Lee (North Korea) is thrown for ippon with Koga's unique one-handed seoi-nage.

Back in Japan he took the amazing decision to enter the All-Japan championships, an open weight competition despite weighting only 71kg, and astonished everyone by making it into the final, defeating opponents twice his size with superior speed and tactics. It took the world open weight champion, Naoya Ogawa, to beat him, and judo in Japan experienced a surge in popularity as a result of this exciting match.

But Barcelona was to provide Koga with his greatest moments. In 1991 he won the world championships with another fantastic display of virtuoso judo, defeating Ruiz, the Spanish home favourite, in the final, and it was there in 1992 that he became Olympic champion. Incredibly, Koga won the Games carrying a knee injury that practically prevented him walking, let alone fighting. Immediately prior to his first fight he had anti-inflammatory solution injected into his knee six times. This, and pure guts, helped him make it through to another series of injections, and the final, which he won by decision against Bertalan Hajtos of Hungary. Koga recalls: 'While I was waiting for that decision it was like walking in hell. I was in agony during the wait. But when the three flags rose in my favour it felt like I had suddenly been transported to heaven.' After Barcelona he retired from competition for a couple of years, but returned fresh and highly motivated at the higher weight of -78kg to win the 1995 world championships in front of his home crowd in Makuhari with the maximum 5 ippon wins.

Koga throws Djamel Bouras (France) for Ippon with his own invention – a wrong shoulder sode-tsuri-komi-goshi. Semi-final, 1995 World Championships, Makuhari, Japan.

The next year, in Atlanta, he just failed to take his second Olympic title, losing to Djamel Bouras of France, by a decision.

Koga's personal maxim is 'a new wind'. He says: 'I believe you should always have an open mind when it comes to adopting new approaches and new ways of tackling problems. I want this fresh wind blowing through my heart and mind as I face up to the challenge of my latest goal.'

58

MARIE-CLAIRE RESTOUX

DOB **9 April 1968**
COUNTRY **France**
WEIGHT **-52kg**
HEIGHT **1.67m 5ft 6ins**
OCCUPATION

BEST RESULTS

Olympic Games
Atlanta 1996 gold

World Championships
Makuhari 1995 gold
Paris 1997 gold
Birmingham 1999 bronze

European Championships
Den Haag 1996 bronze
Ostende 1997 bronze
Oviedo 1998 bronze

FAVOURITE TECHNIQUES
Left osoto-gari, left tsuri-goshi, tani-otoshi, juji-gatame

MARIE-CLAIRE RESTOUX was the darling of French judo. With a twinkle in her eye and an impish look she won two world titles and the 1996 Olympic title. Competing at the same time as the massive David Douillet the petite 52kg fighter was his total opposite, but between them they were perfect ambassadors for French Judo.

When Restoux took her first world title in 1995 it was a major surprise. The young pretty fighter had not been seen outside France but showed no respect for anyone, smashing Wang of China with an ouchi-gari leg grab in the semi-final and armlocking Carolin Mariani of Argentina with juji-gatame to take the title.

By Atlanta the world was ready for her. She fought at the European championships in May of the same year and lost against the 1992 Olympic Champion, Almudena Munoz (Spain), by decision. In the bronze match she produced a superb osoto-gari ippon on the Polish fighter Krause.

But she had been recorded and analysed by everyone and it looked as though the world title might have been a flash in the pan. Restoux proved to be the fighter for the big occasion, twitching Pedulla (USA) with kosoto-gari for waza-ari and defeating Krause again in the semi-final, though only by decision. The final against the strong Korean fighter Sook-hee Hyun was decided by two exciting exchanges. In the first Restoux attacked across the body and Hyun blocked and countered strongly with ura-nage. Switching direction the Frenchwoman rode the Korean's counter to the mat – she had countered the counter for yuko. Hyun came back strongly and caught Restoux sweetly with an incredibly fast ashi-guruma. Restoux went over like a rocket desperately twisting in the air, landing hard and fast, but virtually on her front for a koka. Restoux hung on to become Olympic champion and took a flying leap off the mat into the arms of her coach!

At the Paris world championships Restoux was back to defend her title. Interestingly she had never performed well on home ground, failing to make any impression in the Tournoi de Paris. With the famous French crowd behind her she turned on the style flattening Mariani (Argentina) with a travelling ouchi leg grab that sent the crowd wild! The final was against Sun-hui Kye of North Korea who, aged 16, had amazingly defeated Ryoko Tamura of Japan in the -48kg final in Atlanta. Kye had moved up to the -52kg and, supremely confident, stood between Restoux and her third major title.

The two Olympic Champions produced a great world final. Though Restoux had the crowd behind her Kye looked the stronger. Early in the fight she sent Restoux flying with a left tai-otoshi for waza-ari. Desperately she fought a rear-guard action. Both fighters were penalised to chui, and when Kye received keikoku for a false attack there was a glimmer of hope. The North Korean seemed to mistakenly assume that the scores were level and came pressing forward looking to score. With seconds to go Restoux seized her chance and picked her off, faking to the front and then driving her backwards to score waza-ari. Both fighters were unsure of the score and it was not until the fight was awarded that the familiar jaunty smile appeared on the face of Restoux. It was a famous victory snatched from the jaws of defeat.

ANGELIQUE SERIESE

DOB **12 July 1968**
COUNTRY **Netherlands**
WEIGHT **+72kg**
HEIGHT **1.80m 5ft 11ins**
OCCUPATION **Office administrator**

BEST RESULTS

Olympic Games
Seoul 1988 gold

World Championship
Essen 1987 bronze
Hamilton 1993 silver
Makuhari 1995 gold

European Championships
Paris 1987 silver
Pamplona 1988 gold
Helsinki 1989 gold (+72g)/gold (Open)
Prague 1991 bronze
Paris 1992 gold (Open)
Athens 1993 gold (Open)
Gdansk 1994 gold
Birmingham 1995 gold (Open)
Den Haag 1996 gold

Tournoi de Paris
1988 silver
1989 gold

FAVOURITE TECHNIQUES
Makikomi and combinations, including a form of tani-otoshi; osoto-gari. kansetsu-waza, osaeokomi

ANGELIQUE SERIESE first made her impact on international competition at the age of 19, a young age for a heavyweight, when she won a silver at the European championships in Paris in 1987, beaten by the more experienced French champion, Isabelle Paque. 'It encouraged me because I felt that I came so close and I could win the Europeans,' she said. It happened the following year.

When she was still only 19, in the European championships in Pamplona, she found herself in the final against Paque again – and this time she won. Shortly after her 20th birthday, she went to the Seoul Olympics where women's judo was represented for the first time, and won unexpectedly.

'I was against Fenglian Gao, the large Chinese and everyone thought she was unbeatable,' recalled Seriese. 'That made it all the more of a challenge for me.' The fight was a battle of gripping as both were makikomi specialists. Seriese also liked newaza but was warned that the Chinese opponent was so strong it would be inadvisable to go to the ground. It was well into the match by the time that Seriese realised her ground work was a match for Gao's – too late to produce a decisive score. But the Dutch champion won on a clear decision.

It was one of the high points in Seriese's career matched only by the two golds – heavyweight and Open – that she won the following year in the European championships in Helsinki.

But that year saw her suffer her first serious knee injury – the bane of judo fighters – and it put her out of competition for a year. The remaining goal, then, was the world title which eluded her. She tried in 1991, but came fifth. She tried again in Hamilton in 1993, but pulled a hamstring in the semi-final and could scarcely defend against Beata Maksymow (Poland) in the final and had to be satisfied with silver.

Olympic Games Final, Seoul 1988 versus Fenglian Gao (China).

Finally, in 1995, in Makuhari in Japan, she achieved her goal, nearly armlocking her Chinese opponent, though finally winning on decision.

As she made an impact on international competition so young, she was still keen to continue despite having won all the major championships. But though she won the European championships again in 1996, she lost to Germany's Joanna Hagn in the Atlanta Olympics in 1996. And the following year, further injuries made it sensible to retire.

'I love the sport, but it was not smart to go on – I would have had trouble as I got older,' she explained.

Seriese continued to train at Chris de Korte's club in Rotterdam – which also produced other outstanding fighters, including 2000 Olympic Champion Mark Huizinga – but stopped in 2001. 'I was playing, and I am afraid I did not find it easy to play at a sport where I was accustomed to win.' At the time of writing, Seriese was looking for another sport to absorb her interest.

EMMANUELLA PIERANTOZZI

DOB **22 August 1968**
TOWN/COUNTRY **Bologna, Italy**
WEIGHT **-66kg -78kg**
HEIGHT **1.77m 5ft 10.5ins**
OCCUPATION **Sports science teacher and trainer**

BEST RESULTS

Olympic Games
Barcelona 1992 silver
Sydney 2000, bronze (-78kg)

World Championships
Belgrade 1989 gold
Barcelona 1991 gold
Paris 1997 bronze

European Championships
Pamplona 1988 silver
Helsinki 1989 gold
Prague 1991 bronze
Paris 1992 gold
Athens 1993 bronze
Birmingham 1995 silver
Den Haag 1996 silver

Tournoi de Paris
1991 gold
1999 gold (-78kg)

Fukuoka Championships
1989 gold

World Student Games
1991 gold

FAVOURITE TECHNIQUES
Uchimata, osoto-gari, ouchi-gari, tani-otoshi, juji-gatame, sangaku-gatame, okuri-eri-jime

TALL, POWERFUL and aggressive, Emmanuella Pierantozzi was a dominant figure in the late 1980s and early 1990s. Fighting spirit was her strongest weapon – she never gave up – and the long arm reaching over for a strong grip was a warning to all opponents of a dangerous uchimata, ouchi-gari or osoto-gari. There was no hiding place on the ground either, with armlocks and strangles always threatening.

Among her most memorable matches was her nine-second win against the German champion Alexandra Schreiber in the semi-final of the Barcelona Olympics. 'Before the fight I thought about what I should do – it was very important to me to win, because it meant the Olympic final,' remembered Pierantozzi.

'Even though she knew me, and we had fought before, I thought I should surprise her. So I took hold and pushed her back hard and she reacted, pushing against me. I turned in for uchimata, and it was over, in nine seconds.'

By this time, Pierantozzi was an established, mature competitor. But when she first made an impression in international judo, in the European championships in 1988 where she won a silver (beaten by Schreiber) she was a very different judoka. 'I wasn't really trained. I was physically fit, but I had to rely on my instinct. This instinct for judo, for what to do in a competition, was more intelligent than me.'

In particular, Pierantozzi remarks that she had a natural talent for feeling what her opponent was going to do, and when her opponent was strong or weak. One of her key matches was on the way to her first European title in 1998. She faced Claire Lecat (France), and the French champion went ahead with a yuko. But halfway into the fight, Pierantozzi suddenly realized that Lecat, whom she admits was better trained than herself, was weakening, and she doubled her attacking rate and won. 'I

Olympic Games Semi-Final, Barcelona 1992. Uchimata ippon in nine seconds on Alexandra Schreiber (Germany).

won because I wanted to win.' In the final, she beat Schreiber.

Pierantozzi started judo at the age of nine because 'I had a lot of energy and enthusiasm.' She did other sports as she grew up, but judo was her principal interest. She won her first national judo championships at 13, and although she stopped from 15 to 18 with knee problems – she was growing fast – she won again almost immediately after she returned.

The heat of the battle attracted her then and still attracts her now. Those years between 1989 and 1992 when she was at her peak were memorable. In the world championships in 1991 at Barcelona, she won her second title with four ippons and a yuko – ending with the sangaku roll into osaekomi against Jimenes Reve of Cuba.

Despite more uneven medal success since, with absences caused by injury and other problems, she remains a strong adversary as she proved when she returned in 1999 to compete in the Tournoi de Paris and a host of other 'A' tournaments in the -78kg category; and then took a bronze in the Olympic Games in Sydney. She was older, and more tactical, but the same basic desire to win brought her more medal success.

Although now in her thirties, she is still not sure whether she is ready to retire. 'I love judo. It is very interesting, in that you are fighting not only physically but mentally. And from judo you can learn how to live.'

DAVID DOUILLET

DOB **17 February 1969**

TOWN/COUNTRY **Neufchatel en Bray, Normandy, France**

WEIGHT **+95kg / +100kg / Open; actual weight 130kg**

HEIGHT **1.96m 6ft 5ins**

OCCUPATION **Appointed French heavyweight coach 2001**

BEST RESULTS

Olympic Games
Barcelona 1992 bronze (+95kg)
Atlanta 1996 gold (+95kg)
Sydney 2000 gold (+100kg)

World Championships
Hamilton 1993 gold (+95kg)
Makuhari 1995 gold (+95kg)
Makuhari 1995 gold (Open)
Paris 1997 gold (+95kg)

European Championships
Prague 1991 bronze (+95kg)
Paris 1992 bronze (+95kg)
Athens 1993 silver (+95kg)
Gdansk 1994 gold (+95kg)

Tournoi de Paris
1993 bronze (+95kg)
1995 silver (+95kg)

Mediterranean Games
Bari 1997 gold (+95kg)

TECHNIQUES
Right uchimata, right harai-goshi, right ouchi-gari, right osoto-gari

WHEN DAVID DOUILLET won the controversial final fight of the 2000 Sydney Olympics he became the most successful international judoka of all time, overtaking Yasuhiro Yamashita's record. The first fighter to win four world and two Olympic gold medals became a sporting superstar in France and gave judo the highest profile it had ever achieved outside Japan.

Aged six Douillet sat watching TV as Jean-Luc Rougé won the world title for France in Vienna in 1975. Beside Douillet were his comics. The Adventures of Dr Justice had introduced him to the mystical power of the martial arts, and now a Frenchman was beating the best fighters in the world. The next year French hurdler Guy Drut, won Olympic gold in Montreal, and gave Douillet his first glimpse of Olympic glory. But it was four years later, when he saw the awesome opening of the 1980 Moscow Games, he decided this was the stage on which he wished to compete. At 11, he joined his local judo club in Neufchatel en Bray. Douillet remembers how his coach in Neufchatel, Jaques Lemaitre, passed on his passion for judo to his pupils: 'You progress thanks to that passion. You can suffer the huge quantity of training you have to endure because of passion.' He trained twice a week, but at 15 he enrolled at the Lycée Sports-Etudes, a specialist sports school in Rennes, where he could train twice a day: 'My teachers at school in Neufchatel wanted me to slow down in my judo and concentrate on my academic studies. They wanted to scare me – a bunch of short-sighted scribblers who, fortunately, didn't influence me.'

He became French cadet champion at 17 and his coach at Rennes, Serge Decoster, decided he should move to Paris, to the French national training centre, INSEP. Here, as a 17 year-old, Douillet learned to suffer. He remembers one particularly vicious fighter who humiliated him daily. 'It was purgatory. If I met him on the tatami today I would behead him.'

In 1989 at Athens he took the bronze in the European junior championships. In 1990 he underlined his potential in London, defeating some of the top international heavyweights: Elvis Gordon (Great Britain), Harry van Barneveld (Belgium) and Bjarni Fridriksson (Iceland), to win the British Open. In 1991, aged 22, he took a bronze medal in the Prague European championships and, at Barcelona, fought in his first world championships. In his second fight he was strangled by Frank Moreno of Cuba, and came up against van Barneveld again, losing by an osoto-gari for yuko in the repechage. The next year he was back in Barcelona for his first Olympics. He threw Elvis Gordon, Henry Stohr (Germany) and Ernesto Perez (Spain) before meeting world champion Naoya Ogawa (Japan) in the semi-final. Ogawa bowled him over with left tai-otoshi, and Douillet fought for bronze against the Cuban, Moreno.

With a few seconds to go, he was narrowly behind, and launched a brilliant last ditch harai-makikomi, scoring yuko. Afterwards he said: 'I put everything into that last attack. I am very proud to have won, and to have proved that I have it in me.'

From then on there was no stopping Douillet. The next year in Canada he stormed through everyone to take his first world title, defeating the Olympic champion David Khakhaleichvili (Georgia) in the final. Trailing by waza-ari at the last matte, with six seconds to go, the big Georgian smiled and raised his thumb to the Frenchman, conceding defeat. Douillet had arrived at the top!

Two years later, at the 1995 world championships in Japan, he went for the double: +95kg and the Open. On fantastic form, he took both titles, throwing Frank Moller (Germany) with a hooking ouchi leg-grab in the +95kg, and sweeping Sergei Kosorotov (Russia) into kami-shiho-gatame to take the Open. Both victories were celebrated with a triumphant jump into the air.

At the 1996 Atlanta Olympics he was favourite to take the title, and he did not disappoint, taking revenge in the semi-final on Ogawa for his 1992 Olympic defeat with a yuko from ouchi gari. In the final it took him less than a minute to dispose of Ernesto Perez with a right hopping uchimata, celebrated with the now famous jump.

Already the most successful European judoka , he equalled Yasuhiro Yamashita's all-time record the next year at home in Paris. In the +100kg world final, after a flurry of ashiwaza attacks, he went ahead by virtue of a chui given to his opponent, Shinichi Shinohara (Japan). Both fighters were then repeatedly penalised for passivity until Shinohara received hansoku-make – disqualification.

Many felt the decision unjust, but this was nothing by comparison with the outcry that followed the final match of the 2000 Sydney Olympics. Shinohara had captured the +100kg and open weight world titles in Great Britain the year before. But against the odds, Douillet made a comeback to full fitness for Sydney. He defeated Tataroglu (Turkey), van Barneveld (Belgium) and Pertelson (Estonia), all by ippon, on his way to the final against Shinohara.

In the decisive incident of the fight Douillet attacked with uchimata. As Shinohara fell to the mat he attempted to counter the Frenchman. Douillet fell on his back as Shinohara landed on his side. Douillet was awarded yuko, and scored another yuko from a counter-attack later in the fight, to take his second Olympic title.

Outrage from Japanese supporters followed; their belief was that Shinohara had countered Douillet for ippon. The IJF examined the video evidence, and concluded that no score should have been given either way. It was the most debated judo incident of all time.

Douillet does the double! World Championships, Makuhari 1995.

But Douillet, the supreme competitor, left competitive judo in the best possible way, an Olympic champion again. He admitted to a tinge of sadness, explaining that a chapter of his life had closed. The record books will show David Douillet of France as the first judoka to win four world and two Olympic titles, and the famous celebratory leap of the mighty Frenchman has become an enduring memory in the history of judo.

NAZIM GOUSSEINOV

DOB **2 August 1969**
TOWN/COUNTRY **Baku, Azerbaijan**
WEIGHT **-60kg**
HEIGHT **5ft 6ins, 1.68m**

BEST RESULTS

Olympic Games
Barcelona 1992 gold

World Championships
Barcelona 1991 bronze
Hamilton 1993 silver

European Championships
Paris 1992 gold
Athens 1993 gold

FAVOURITE TECHNIQUES
Uchimata, harai-goshi, ashi-guruma, sasae-tsuri-komi-ashi, bear-hug kosoto-gari, Khabarelli pick-up

NAZIM GOUSSEINOV was the Soviet Union's -60kg fighter when the Union dissolved and the separate states began competing in their own right. Originating from the small state of Azerbaijan, between the Caucasus Mountains and the Caspian Sea, Gousseinov replaced 1989 world champion Amiran Totikashvilli from Georgia as the Soviet Union's lightweight when he took a world bronze medal in 1991.

Unlike most fighters from the Caucasus region, his major scoring techniques were not power based. Instead he displayed astonishing agility and gymnastic poise to explode into beautiful right-handed uchimata and ashi-guruma, often adopting an unusual reverse right handed lapel-grip, which confused his opponents. He refined the entry into the Khabarelli pick-up, using it as a direct attack and as a counter to head-on attacks. With a right-footed sasae-tsuri-komi-ashi and a bear-hug-style right kosoto-gari, he was a complete standing fighter, with a 360 degree range of world-class attacks.

By contrast, and almost uniquely amongst top class fighters, he had no newaza. He routinely gave up positions of considerable advantage on the ground to continue fighting in tachi-waza. But he was rarely beaten on the ground, as his opponents found it almost impossible to take him down.

He first appeared, fighting for the Soviet Union, at the 1991 Barcelona world championships. In round two, against Chen of China, he produced one of the best throws of the tournament, an incredibly fast ippon-scoring harai-goshi that became uchimata in mid-throw and had both men a metre off the ground!

He lost in the semi-final to Tadanori Koshino of Japan, by a solitary koka, but then threw Israel Hernandez of Cuba with uchimata ippon to take the bronze. The 1992 European championships were held at the Coubertin stadium in Paris and he threw Phillippe Pradayrol of France for ippon with ashi-guruma in the face of his opponent's home crowd to take the title.

At the Barcelona Olympics, the Soviet Union had disappeared and Gousseinov appeared for the Unified team. He made no mistakes, and his semi-final with Koshino was the most exciting match of the entire championships, with both fighters committed to all-out attack. First one led, then the other. One ashi-guruma attack by Gousseinov was scored ippon by the referee and down-graded to yuko by the judges. The fight was decided by a Khabarelli counter to Koshino's leg-grab, which landed the Japanese in a bridge and scored Gousseinov waza-ari. In the final he faced Hyun Yoon of Korea, and threw him for koka with a totally committed combination of hiza-guruma and uranage, to take the Olympic title.

By 1993 he was fighting for Azerbaijan in its own right, and won the Athens European championships, defeating former team-mate Khasin Bisoultanov of Russia in the final. At the Hamilton world championships he destroyed a series of world-class fighters, including Nigel Donohue of Great Britain, Natik Bagirov of Belarussia and Georgi Vazagashvili of Georgia, en route to the final against Ryuji Sonoda of Japan. He led the fight with an ashiwaza for yuko but lost to Sonoda's osoto-gari waza-ari. The two were to fight again, for the bronze in the 1995 Makuhari world championships, and there, for the first time on the international stage, Gousseinov was taken to the ground and held down for ippon.

But it is for the glorious summer in 1992 in Barcelona that he will be remembered, especially by his newly independent compatriots. In the last fight of the Olympics he became the first Azerbaijani to win an Olympic gold medal.

Gousseinov's flying uchimata.
World Championships, Barcelona 1991.

Olympic Games final, Atlanta 1996. Throwing Kim (Korea) with seoi-nage.

PAWEL NASTULA

DOB **26 June 1970**
TOWN/COUNTRY **Warsaw, Poland**
WEIGHT **-95kg / -100kg**
HEIGHT **1.80m 6ft 0ins**
OCCUPATION **Fitness centre proprietor**

BEST RESULTS

Olympic Games
Atlanta 1996 gold

World Championships
Barcelona 1991 silver
Makuhari 1995 gold
Paris 1997 gold

European Championships
Gdansk 1994 gold
Birmingham 1995 gold
Den Haag 1996 gold
Bratislava 1999 silver (-100k)

FAVOURITE TECHNIQUES
Left ippon-seoi-nage, kuchiki-taoshi, juji-gatame, sangaku-gatame

PRINCIPAL PUBLICATIONS
Moje Judo

TWICE SPORTS personality of the year in Poland, Pawel Nastula was an unknown 21 year old when he displayed formidable skills to reach the final of the 1991 world championships. He produced a brilliant throw on Jiri Sosna (Czechoslovakia) in the semi-final. Losing by waza-ari, with 37 seconds left, he tucked under him with left ippon-seoi-nage, only gripping the sleeve end, and planted him firmly on his back. He lost in the final to the juji-gatame armlock of Frenchman Stephane Traineau.

At the 1992 Olympics, Nastula had an excellent run to the semi-final, defeating Yoon (Korea) and ending the career of the great Belgian Robert Van de Walle, throwing them both for ippon with his running leg-grab. A seoi-nage ippon on Baljinnyam (Mongolia) followed before a decision loss to the Briton Ray Stevens. In the bronze medal fight he had the first of many hard battles against Dimitri Sergeev (Russia) and was beaten with an ouchi leg-grab for waza-ari. Sergeev also eliminated him from the 1993 world championships.

But the next year's European event was held in Gdansk, Poland. In front of his home crowd Nastula turned on the style, taking revenge on Stevens (Britain) by pinning him in the final. Nastula had reached the top. Internationally, Europe completely dominated the -95kg category, taking all the medals and seven of the top eight Olympic places. Victory in Europe represented the number 1 spot in the world.

Nastula reigned supreme in the category until the weights changed four years later. To the running leg-grab and left ippon-seoi-nage he added superb tactics. Always cool, he knew exactly when to press forward and wind up the pressure, and when to break the flow. When his opponent started to dominate, Nastula's belt would come undone or his knee required treatment. The 'Nastula rest' with about 90 seconds to go was legendary, and he became known as 'the canny Pole'. Once ahead he would take the fight to the ground, producing a series of progressive newaza moves that ate up the time to the bell.

In the 1995 European final against Sergeev, Nastula fought one of the longest and most enthralling newaza battles in judo's recent history. Leading by shido, Nastula went to the ground to avoid another standing loss to the Russian. For the rest of the contest he switched back and forth between juji-gatame attempts and uki-gatame hold-downs. He achieved osaekomi twice, one of them scoring yuko. When the clock ran out they had been continuously in newaza for two minutes and fifty seconds! Nastula retained his title, and finally defeated Sergeev. In 1995 he beat him again to become world champion in Japan.

At the 1996 Olympics Nastula was overwhelming favourite. He beat reigning Olympic champion, Antal Kovacs (Hungary) with juji-gatame, countered the uchimata of Luigi Guido (Italy) for ippon, and threw Pedro Soares (Portugal) with left ippon-seoi-nage for another maximum score.

Another master tactician, Aurelio Miguel of Brazil wound him up to keikoku in the semi-final and looked set for victory, but with 19 seconds left the Pole clawed himself back with a desperate kosoto-gari counter to the Brazilian's ouchi-gari and won the match. In the final he overwhelmed Kim (Korea), dropping under him with left ippon-seoi-nage, catching him on his back, rising again to turn him over with right seoi-nage, and following into mune-gatame to score ippon.

The -95kg category was contested for the last time at the 1997 world championships, which provided Nastula's last great day. His amazing uranage-style counter on Daniel Guerschner (Germany) was one of the throws of the tournament.

In the final he again faced Brazil's Aurelio Miguel. In a fight between two great tacticians both scored yuko and both were penalised to keikoku. There was nothing to separate them, and Nastula won a split decision.

He now had to decide whether to drop five kilos to the new -90kg category, or gain five kilos and compete in the -100kg and opted for the heavier weight, though it did not suit him. In the Sydney Olympics he was foot-swept for ippon by Ariel Zeevi (Israel) in his first fight. It was an unfitting end to the great career of the canny Pole.

DAVID KHAKHALEICHVILI

DOB **28 February 1971**
TOWN/COUNTRY **Gori, Georgia**
WEIGHT **+95kg / Open**
HEIGHT **1.88m 6ft 2ins**

BEST RESULTS

Olympic Games
Barcelona 1992 gold (+95kg)

World Championships
Barcelona 1991 silver (Open)
Hamilton 1993 silver (+95kg)

European Championships
Athens 1993 gold (+95kg)
Athens 1993 gold (Open)
Den Haag 1996 gold (+95kg)

Junior European Championships
Vienna 1988 gold (+95kg)
Athens 1989 gold (+95kg)

FAVOURITE TECHNIQUES
Ogoshi, uchimata, uki-goshi

THE SMALL country of Georgia has supplied many of the Soviet Union's most feared competitors, including Shota Khabarelli, Amiran Totikashvili and Bashir Varaev. But the first to be recognised as Georgian on the international stage was David Khakhaleichvili. A huge bear of a man, Khakhaleichvili's judo was typical of his region. A strong right grip over the shoulder or on the belt was followed by huge hip-throws – ogoshi, uki-goshi and tsuri-goshi. He also favoured tai-otoshi and a big uchimata.

At the 1988 European junior championships he won the +95kg, for the Soviet Union. The following year he won again. The bronze medallist that day was David Douillet of France, who would be a rival for many years. At the 1990 European event, as a senior, he lost the first round to counter-attack expert, Elvis Gordon of Great Britain, but won all his repecharge fights by ippon to take bronze. With unrest in Georgia, to further his judo career, Khakhaleichvili moved to Japan to train and work, employed by the Sato Kogyo company.

At the Barcelona world championships, he reached the final against the defending champion, Japan's Naoya Ogawa, who had lost to the other Soviet heavyweight, Sergei Kosorotov in the +95kg, and needed to re-establish his superiority. Half-way through, he bowled Khakhaleichvili over with left tai-otoshi for ippon.

By the 1992 Olympics Khakhaleichvilli had dismissed the home challenge of the Russian Kosorotov, and was the surprise Unified team +95kg entry. Unstoppable, he pinned Diouf (Senegal), threw Frank Moreno (Cuba) with harai-makikomi, defeated Rafael Kubacki (Poland) by koka, and threw Imre Csosz (Hungary) with tai-otoshi for waza-ari. The final was a re-run of the 1991 world event, and Ogawa was favourite. But the Georgian hadn't read the script. Straight away he threw his right arm over Ogawa's shoulder and launched a huge tsuri-goshi scoring waza-ari. Less than a minute later his arm was over Ogawa's back again, gripping the shoulder, but instead of throwing forwards, he launched himself in the opposite direction with tani-otoshi, to score waza-ari-awasate-ippon, and take the title. It was all over in 1 minute 24 seconds. The Georgian flag was raised at the medal ceremony and Khakhaleichvili said: 'It is an historic moment because, until now, we have never seen the Georgian flag hoisted at an international tournament.'

Competing for Georgia at the 1993 European championships Khakhaleichvili won the Open and +95kg titles. The same year, at the worlds, he took silver in the +95kg, losing by waza-ari to David Douillet. Sergei Kosorotov (Russia) took the bronze, whilst Estonia's Indrek Pertelson came fifth, underlining the depth of former Soviet talent.

Throughout 1994 and 1995, Khakhaleichvili gained weight and looked past his best whenever he fought. But he came back with a vengeance at the 1996 European championships in Holland. Trimmed down in size, he demolished Csosz (Hungary) with ogoshi in the semi-final, and defeated Kosorotov with osoto-gari for yuko to take the +95kg title and claim his Olympic place. Absent from Holland was David Douillet, who now had three world titles. The potential Olympic clash between European and Olympic Champion Khakhaleichvili, and world champion Douillet, was eagerly anticipated.

Unfortunately, it was not to be. On the first day of the 1996 Olympic Games in Atlanta, in a shocking mix-up, Khakhaleichvili was given the wrong directions to the weigh-in, got lost in the traffic, failed to get to the weigh-in on time, and was not allowed to compete. It was a sad end to a great career.

Olympic Games final, Barcelona 1992. Already leading by waza-ari Khakhaleichvili launches a massive ko-soto-gari against Naoya Ogawa (Japan) to score waza-ari awasate ippon and take the title.

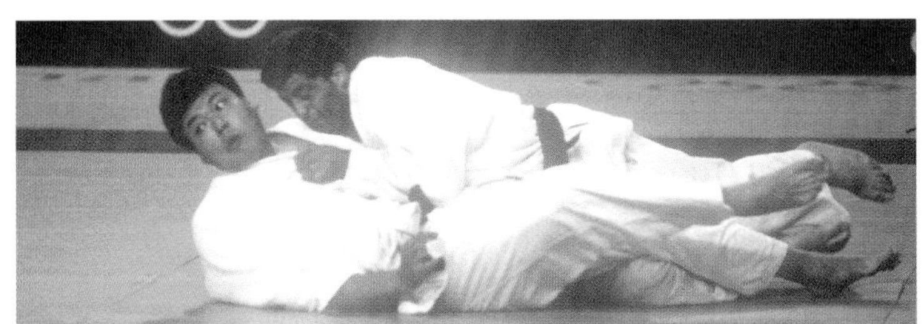

Olympic Games final, Atlanta 1996. Countering Yoko Tanabe (Japan) for ippon with uchimata sukashi.

ULLA WERBROUCK

DOB **24 January 1972**
TOWN/COUNTRY **Izegem, Belgium**
WEIGHT **-66kg / -72kg / -70kg**
HEIGHT **1.79m 5ft 10ins**
OCCUPATION **Judoka**

ULLA WERBROUCK took over from Ingrid Berghmans as the Belgian to be feared in the -72kg category. An upright fighter with a beautiful right uchimata as her tokui-waza she has helped make judo one of Belgium's most popular sports. Werbrouck started judo in 1983, aged 11, at her local club in Izegem. Five years later she won the first of three junior European titles. In 1989 she fought in her first senior European event, slimming down to -66kg to avoid Berghmans, and took a bronze. In 1990 she won the world junior championships in Dijon and her first senior European medal at -72kg, a bronze in Frankfurt, armlocking the Yugoslav Blagosevic with juji-gatame.

Under the guidance of her charismatic national coach Jean-Marie Dedecker and the former Soviet trainer, Alexander Iatskevitch, she visibly hardened as a fighter, and the breakthrough came in 1994, in Gdansk, when she took her first European gold medal, defeating Estha Essombe (FRA). For the next six years she reigned supreme in Europe, taking six titles in a row.

At the Makuhari world championships, the Japanese persuaded light heavyweight Yoko Tanabe to come out of retirement. Tanabe had been the principal rival of Berghmans and had beaten Werbrouck in the 1991 Fukuoka Cup. She was her mirror image, strong and upright but with a left handed uchimata. Throughout her career Werbrouck would rate Tanabe as her toughest opponent. In Makuhari they met in the semi-final and in a very close fought match the Belgian won, scoring koka with tani-otoshi. In the final she faced the powerful, scrappy Cuban Luna Castellano who kept up a relentless pace and prevented Werbrouck from scoring. At full time the Cuban pinched it on a split decision. It was the most disappointing defeat of Werbrouck's career but spurred her on to train even harder for the Atlanta Olympics.

BEST RESULTS

Olympic Games
Atlanta 1996 gold
Sydney 2000 5th (-70kg)

World Championships
Makuhari 1995 silver
Paris 1997 bronze
Birmingham 1999 silver (-70kg)

European Championships
Helsinki 1989 bronze (-66)
Frankfurt 1990 bronze
Prague 1991 bronze
Paris 1992 silver
Athens 1993 silver
Gdansk 1994 gold
Birmingham 1995 gold
Den Haag 1996 gold
Ostende 1997 gold
Oviedo 1998 gold
Bratislava 1999 gold
Wroclaw 2000 bronze
Paris 2001 gold

Junior World Championships
Dijon 1990 gold

Junior European Championships
Vienna 1988 gold
Athens 1989 gold
Ankara 1990 gold

FAVOURITE TECHNIQUES
Right uchimata, right osoto-gari, juji-gatame

European Final, Ostende 1997. Ulla Werbrouck throws Chloe Cowen (Great Britain) for Ippon with a massive right uchimata.

At the Games the draw was in her favour. The big guns of the category, Tanabe, Essombe, Luna and Howey of Great Britain were all in the other half. Werbrouck produced one of the best throws of the tournament in the semi-final, flattening Beliaeva (UKR) for ippon with a massive uchimata. Tanabe won the other half and the stage was set for a classic final. The best of Asia against the best of Europe and two fighters that could really throw. Werbrouck was ready for everything Tanabe could throw at her. She waited and the first left uchimata the Japanese launched she countered for yuko with tani-otoshi. It was a devastating blow for Tanabe. Werbrouck's uchimata, when it came, was deeper and more committed. Tanabe twisted in mid air and kept the score down to yuko. Her next attack was countered again. She had to come forward and tried left uchimata for the third time. Werbrouck neatly side stepped and planted her on her back with uchimata sukashi for ippon. Werbrouck was champion.

Atlanta was the high point of her career. She was a Belgian heroine when they hosted the European championships in Ostende the following year. In the midst of numerous Belgian victories, in front of a packed stadium, she threw Britain's Chloe Cowen with a massive uchimata that sent the audience wild. It was one of the greatest moments in European judo.

After such great exploits many would have retired, but Werbrouck had not yet taken a world title and wanted to put her name into the record books as European, world and Olympic Champion. A decision loss to Essombe in 1997 left her with the bronze, and she was thrown in the 1999 final for ippon by the new young Cuban Sibelis Veranes. But in 2000 she won the Tournoi de Paris, defeating Min-Sun Cho (KOR) with a phenomenal uchimata. She was unable to repeat that form at the 2000 Sydney Olympics and Cho turned the tables, defeating Werbrouck for the bronze medal.

Incredibly, 2001 saw her back to her best, taking her seventh European title. 'Not bad for an old woman!' she said afterwards, 'I'm still enjoying myself, so I'm going to keep going. Besides, I've won everything except the world championships, so I've got to have another try at that!'

MIN-SUN CHO

DOB **21 March 1972**

TOWN/COUNTRY **Youngam-gun, Jeollanam-do, Korea**

WEIGHT **-48kg / -52kg / -56kg / -66kg / -70kg**

HEIGHT **1.74m 5ft 8ins**

OCCUPATION **Graduate student**

MIN-SUN CHO was Korea's greatest woman fighter. She was unstoppable in the -66kg, winning two world gold medals and the Olympic title. Her weapons were a driving left ouchi-gari leg-grab, and her favourite technique, a dynamic left uchimata.

She first appeared at -48kg, taking the bronze at the 1988 Olympics. She went up to -52kg for the 1989 world event, taking another bronze and, at -56kg, won the 1990 world junior championships. Three years later, now at -66kg, she defeated everyone at the 1993 world championships with left ouchi-gari, including Olympic champion, Odalys Reve-Jiminez of Cuba who attacked her with kosoto-gari, only to be countered with the ouchi. In the final she destroyed the American Liliko Ogasawa with the ouchi-gari, dropping her left arm over the shoulder for ippon.

In 1995 in Makuhari, she successfully defended her title. This time left uchimata was the dominant technique, dispatching Dubois (France) and Ishibashi (Japan). In the semi-final she showed the strength of her newaza, defeating Claudia Zwiers (Netherlands) with koshi-jime. In the final the right-handed Cuban Reve-Jiminez could not cope with her technical excellence. Cho won with a stunningly fast uchimata on the edge.

At the Atlanta Olympics, Cho returned to ouchi-gari as her technique. Following through into newaza, she defeated Campos (Brazil), Wang (China), Pina (Dominican Republic) and Zwiers (Netherlands) with the same throw, the last two for ippon.

In the final another dynamic thrower, Ann Szczepanska of Poland, was waiting for her ouchi and countered for yuko. Cho responded with kosoto-gari for waza-ari. The fight went to the ground, and instead of protecting her lead, Cho gambled, launched herself into a tricky turn into mune-gatame, scored waza-ari-awasate-ippon, and clinched the title. Few could believe she had attempted such a risky move in the Olympic final.

BEST RESULTS

Olympic Games
Seoul 1988 bronze (-48kg)
Atlanta 1996 gold (-66kg)
Sydney 2000 bronze (-70kg)

World Championships
Belgrade 1989 bronze (-52kg)
Hamilton 1993 gold (-66kg)
Mahuhari 1995 gold (-66kg)
Paris 1997 bronze (-70kg)

Asian Games
Beijing 1990 bronze (-56kg)
Hiroshima 1994 silver (-66kg)

Asian Championships
Damascus 1988 bronze (-48kg)
Macau 1993 gold (-66kg)
New Delhi 1995 bronze (-66kg)
Osaka 2000 bronze (-70kg)

Tournoi de Paris
1990 gold (-56kg)
1992 gold (-66kg)
1993 bronze (-66kg)
1995 gold (-66kg)
1996 bronze (-66kg)
2000 silver (-70kg)

Fukuoka Tournament
1988 bronze (-48kg)
1993 gold (-66kg)
1996 gold (-66kg)

Junior World Championships
Dijon 1990 gold (-56 kg)

FAVOURITE TECHNIQUES
Ouchi-gari, uchimata

At the Paris world championships, her winning streak ended in the semi-final against the 1992 Olympic bronze medallist Kate Howey (Britain). Since 1993 Howey had been winning medals at -72kg, but unable to beat Belgium's Ulla Werbrouck, had dieted back down. Cho could not match Howey's power and was thrown with the double leg-grab, morote-gari, for a thumping ippon. Howey won the category. Cho took the bronze and retired.

But this was not the end of the story. Two years later, after a poor Korean showing in the world championships, the IJF President, Y.S. Park, persuaded her, with an offer of personal sponsorship, to train for the 2000 Olympics in Sydney. The weights had changed and Cho found herself in the new category of -70kg. Coming up from -66kg was 1997 world champion, Kate Howey. Coming down from -72kg was Olympic Champion Ulla Werbrouck of Belgium, and the 1999 Cuban world champion, Sibelis Veranes. Cho breezed through two rounds, foot-sweeping Scapin (ITA) for yuko and throwing Kouzina (Russia) with uchimata for ippon.

Against Veranes in the semi-final she lost a tight contest by a debatable drop seoi-nage koka. Veranes defeated Howey in the final and Cho fought for bronze. In her last fight Cho, the Atlanta -66kg Olympic gold medallist, faced Werbrouck, the Atlanta -72kg Olympic gold medallist. Werbrouck was expecting the ouchi-gari and uchimata of Cho, and threatened with her own uchimata. In a master stroke, the Korean feinted the left inner attack, got the reaction from the Belgian, and switched to a driving kosoto-gari. Too late Werbrouck attempted to twist out but was thrown for waza-ari. The come-back had resulted in an Olympic bronze medal for Cho in one of the hardest fought categories of the Games.

KI-YOUNG JEON

DOB **11 July 1973**

TOWN/COUNTRY **Cheongju-city, Chungcheongbuk-do, Korea**

WEIGHT **-78k / -86k**

HEIGHT **1.78m 5ft 11ins**

OCCUPATION **Graduate student and Korea national men's team trainer**

BEST RESULTS

Olympic Games
Atlanta 1996 gold (-86kg)

World Championships
Hamilton 1993 gold (-78kg)
Makuhari 1995 gold (-86kg)
Paris 1997 gold (-86kg)

Tournoi de Paris
1993 gold (-78kg)
1994 silver (-78kg)
1997 gold

Sungkop Tournament
Seoul 1995 gold

FAVOURITE TECHNIQUES
Left drop morote-seoi-nage, left osoto-gari, left uchimata

KI-YOUNG JEON was the greatest Korean judo champion. Three times world champion, and Olympic champion in 1996, he dominated the -86kg category. Fit, and left-handed, he had an unstoppable left drop seoi-nage.

As a 12 year, Jeon watched at home on TV as Jae-Yup Kim won a judo gold at the Los Angeles Olympics, and immediately decided he would be a fighter. Weighing 38kg, he got into a school fight with a 78kg boy and beat him. His PE teacher witnessed the brawl, and pulled Jeon aside. Rather than punishing him, he recognised a born fighter and suggested judo classes. When Jeon saw boys with kit bundles slung nonchalantly over their shoulders, he was hooked.

At high school he met the most influential coach in his career, Hyun-Kyu Hwan. Hwan was a hard mentor, and very tough with his students. He taught Ki-Young his trademark technique, the sharp feint into seoi-nage. The snappy flick downwards with the hands momentarily froze his opponents. Hwan taught him not to throw as they froze, but wait until the moment they relaxed, and then hit them with the killer seoi. His first major success in Korea came at 16, when he beat the established junior international Oh-Jung Hwan, and came to the selectors' attention. Jeon followed 1989 world champion Byung-Ju Kim as Korea's representative at -78kg. Kim took an Olympic bronze in 1992, but the same November Jeon beat him by hantei. At the 1993 Tournoi de Paris, Jeon and his countryman Yoon fought their way into an all-Korean final of the 78kg which Jeon won.

At the 1993 world championships the Olympic champion, Japan's Hidehiko Yoshida, was favourite, and despite injuring himself, fought his way into the final. Jeon defeated Olympic silver-medallist, Jason Morris of the USA, and the talented Frenchman, Darcel Yandzi, to claim the other spot. The injured Yoshida could not produce his best and Jeon threw him with seoi-nage for waza-ari, to take the gold. Many wondered what kind of fight it would have been had Yoshida been uninjured.

In Korea the competition in the -78kg category between Kim, Yoon and Jeon was intense, and Yoon and Jeon again reached the final of the 1994 Tournoi de Paris. This time Yoon won. Jeon decided to move from -78kg to -86kg at the same time as Yoshida made the same step. They met again in the most eagerly anticipated final of the 1995 World championships. The odds seemed stacked against Jeon. Yoshida was at his imperious best, uninjured, fighting on home ground in front of a packed crowd. It was a magnificent fight: non-stop attacking from Yoshida was met with great defence by Jeon. Then came the big seoi-nage from the Korean as he dropped under the Japanese fighter. Yoshida rode the attack, but Jeon came back up into an explosive driving osoto-gari planting Yoshida on his back for ippon. For Jeon this was his most memorable fight: 'Yoshida was my hardest adversary; he never stopped attacking, and beating him in Japan was the greatest feeling.'

The next year Jeon was favourite to win the Olympic title in Atlanta and he did not disappoint. Surviving a tight decision against Mark Huizinga of the Netherlands, he produced some stunning ippons – seoi-nage on Despaigne of Cuba, and a spinning uchimata on Germany's Marco Spittka. Before the final against the unknown Uzbek Amin Bagdasarov, his confidence was so high he went through mental rehearsals not of the fight, but of the victory salute that he would give when he won. And win he did, with two waza-ari scores from seoi-nage.

Paris was his final world championships. Once again he was untouchable, defeating Marco Spittka again in the final. He retired at the top, the finest fighter that Korea has yet produced, and took a PHD in sports at Kyung-gi University, before taking up a position as national trainer to the Korean men's team. When asked the reasons for his success he says: 'I was born to be a fighter, I could not stand losing, and I had great support from my mother and sister. My sister trained as a singer and she always came with my mother to support me. Her voice was so unusual that even in the middle of a fight I could hear her, and I knew I could not lose.'

Tournoi de Paris 1997. Ki-young Jeon throws Merkevicius (Lithuania) with his tokui-waza, drop seoi-nage for ippon, dropping right between the legs and then rising and driving forwards to complete the score.

DRIULYS GONZALEZ

DOB **21 September 1973**
TOWN/COUNTRY **Havanna, Cuba**
WEIGHT **-56kg / -57kg**
HEIGHT **1.61m 5ft 3ins**
OCCUPATION **Judoka**

World Championships, Hamilton 1993. Versus Sun-yong Jung (Korea).

FROM THE moment women's judo became an official Olympic sport at Barcelona in 1992 the Cuban women's team have been regular medal winners. The most consistent fighter, taking a medal at three consecutive Olympic Games was the -56kg competitor Driulys Gonzalez.

Cuba has a small judo playing population of only 3,000 fighters, and the strength of their women's team is largely due to the work of their charismatic and colourful coach, big Ronaldo Veitia Valdivie. It is Ronaldo who travels Cuba seeking out the strongest young women to become fighters. It is Ronaldo who oversees the gruelling training and competition schedules in Cuba and Europe. And it is Ronaldo who gets the women dancing samba before competition and sits in the mat side chair when they fight, waging his psychological war with the referees.

Under Ronaldo's instruction Gonzalez became one of the most consistent fighters in the world, taking six Pan-American titles, two world titles and the 1996 Olympic gold medal. Like all the Cuban women she was enormously powerful, supremely fit, and her principal techniques were drop seoi-nage, a strong ouchi-gari and the double leg grab morote-gari. At her first Olympic Games in Barcelona, Gonzalez was only 18 years old but fought her way into the semi-final where she met the home favourite Miriam Blasco (Spain) and was armlocked with juji-gatame in a little over a minute. She took the bronze with a yuko from uchi-mata on Kate Donahoo of the United States.

Over the next four years she was a consistent medal winner on the European A tournament circuit. With Ronaldo at the mat side dictating her attack plan she took bronze in the 1993 World championships and gold at the next world event in 1995 establishing herself as favourite for the Olympic title in Atlanta the following year. Her draw in America was tough; Magali Baton of France in the first round, Jessica Gal of the

BEST RESULTS

Olympic Games
Barcelona 1992 bronze
Atlanta 1996 gold
Sydney 2000 silver

World Championships
Hamilton 1993 bronze
Makuhari 1995 gold
Paris 1997 silver
Birmingham 1999 gold

Pan American Games
Hamilton 1991 gold
Santiago 1995 gold
Winnepeg 1999 gold

Pan American Championships
San Juan 1996 gold
Guadalajara 1997 gold
Santa Domingo 1998 gold

Tournoi de Paris
1993 bronze
1994 silver
1995 bronze
1996 silver
1997 gold
1998 gold
2000 bronze

Fukuoka Tournament
1997 gold
1999 (Jan) gold
1999 (Dec) gold
2000 gold

FAVOURITE TECHNIQUES
Drop seoinage, ouchi-gari, morote-gari

Netherlands in the second and 1993 world champion, Nicola Fairbrother of Great Britain in the third. All three fights went to time with Gonzalez countering Gal for koka and taking decisions off the other two. In the semi-final she faced Chuang Liu of China and wasted no time, throwing her for ippon with ouchi-gari inside twenty seconds. The final was against Sun-yong Jung of Korea. In virtually the first exchange of the fight Gonzalez dropped to her knees catching Jung on her back in right seoi-nage. Rising and driving to her right she whipped the Korean onto her side for yuko.

Non-stop aggressive fighting from both women followed. Ronaldo was at his most expressive in the chair helping Gonzalez to maintain her lead and the yuko proved decisive. Gonzalez was Olympic Champion.

At the 2000 Olympics Gonzalez was expected to become the first female double Olympic gold medalist, having taken the world title again the previous year. But Ronaldo was not in the chair. For indiscretions the previous day, coaching Legna Verdecia to a gold medal he was confined to the stands. Gonzalez made it through to the final against Isabel Fernandez (Spain) whom she had thrown for waza-ari with sode-tsurikomi-goshi in the world final. Fernandez knew she was unlikely to throw the Cuban and played a very cagey match. Without the tactical brain of Ronaldo to guide her, Gonzalez looked lost and went down keikoku to chui.

But judo history will remember the Cuban team of Gonzalez, Ronaldo and the rest of the samba girls, and the flamboyance and excitement they have brought to the sport.

The Motivator at work, big Ronaldo Veitia.

TADAHIRO NOMURA was the fifth judoka to win two Olympic golds. Uniquely he was the first lightweight to achieve this feat.

Nephew of 1972 Olympic Champion Toyakazu Nomura, and a student of Tenri University, Tadahiro was the surprise Japanese entry at the Atlanta Olympics. His performance was brilliant – most onlookers agreed he was the player of the tournament. A fully committed left hander, he threw caution to the wind and hit the opposition with everything. Not having fought in the previous World event Nomura was unseeded so the most exciting fight of the Olympics, against reigning world champion, Oyegin of Russia, happened in round two. It was a clash of styles, the classical Japanese against the unorthodox rugged Russian, but both were big time attackers. At first there was nothing between them, but then the Russian whipped Nomura over with drop seoi-nage for yuko. More drama followed. Dropping onto both knees, Oyegin caught Nomura on his back in kata-guruma and powered up onto his feet. As Oyegin unloaded Nomura twisted and with amazing agility kept the score down to another yuko.

With seconds to go Nomura was heading for an early exit but, with a one handed grip, he spun under Oyegin and launched him with a rolling sode-tsurikomi goshi for waza-ari, the winning score.

Nomura continued to live dangerously and was again losing to Girolamo Giovinazzo (Italy) in the final, when he disappeared through his legs holding only sleeve ends to whip him onto his back with seoi-nage for ippon. Overnight Tadahiro Nomura was a superstar.

A year later, at the Paris world championships, Nomura was the favorite, the man to beat, and demolished everyone, throwing George Revazishvilli (Georgia) with a beautiful drop seoinage to take the title. But a threat to his supremacy had developed in Japan, in the shape of

TADAHIRO NOMURA

DOB **10 December 1974**

TOWN/COUNTRY **Tenri University, Japan**

WEIGHT **-60kg**

HEIGHT **1.63m 5ft 4ins**

OCCUPATION **Post graduate student, Judoka**

BEST RESULTS

Olympic Games
Atlanta 1996 gold
Sydney 2000 gold

World Championships
Paris 1997 gold

Tournoi de Paris
2000 gold

All Japan weight category championships
1996 gold
1997 gold
2000 gold

FAVOURITE TECHNIQUES
Left ippon-seoi-nage,
left drop morote-seoi-nage,
sode-tsurikomi-goshi (Koga style)

World Championships Final, Paris 1997. A simultaneous attack by George Revazishvili (Georgia) is defeated with drop seoi-nage.

the diminutive Kazuhiko Tokuno, and it was he, not Nomura who took the 1999 world slot. Tokuno made it to the final, but was sweetly thrown for ippon by the Cuban fighter Manolo Poulot.

When Nomura was selected for the 2000 Olympics he was again, incredibly, an unseeded fighter! Since Tokuno had fought in Birmingham, Nomura now became the most dangerous floating fighter possible and, unfortunately, he was drawn on the same side of the table as world champion Poulot. They met in the semi-final. In the match that should have been the final between the reigning Olympic champion and the reigning world champion it was extremely close. Both took small scores with Nomura's left seoi-nage yuko slightly better than Poulot's koka. Nomura was in his second Olympic final.

Olympic Games Semi-Final, Sydney 2000. Versus Manolo Poulot (Cuba).

Ippon seoi-nage ippon. Sydney 2000.

The Japanese fans were still celebrating Ryoko Tamura's spectacular victory as Nomura stepped onto the mat to fight the Korean Bu-kyung Jung. The chants of 'Tamura!, Tamura!' changed to 'Nomura!, Nomura!' The fighters bowed, gripped, skipped to the edge and Nomura attacked. The Korean spun through the air, momentarily bridging as he twisted onto his front. The referee's arm shot into the air as he called 'Ippon' and Nomura was Olympic champion again. It had taken 14 seconds!

After his historic victory he admitted that he had been just as nervous for his second Olympic final as he was for his first and added: 'I just tried my best and this time the feeling is even better.' Asked if he would attempt an unprecedented third Olympic title he said that after a break he would think about going on for another Games! But whatever happens he will be remembered, tongue between his teeth, celebrating in Sydney, the most successful lightweight fighter of all time.

RYOKO TAMURA is the planet's most famous judoka. Called 'Yawara' after a cartoon character modelled on her, she is mobbed wherever she goes in Japan and the 'Tamura! Tamura!' chant from her army of fans has been deafening in three Olympic finals.

She deserves her fame. At the time of writing she is 25 years old but already four times world champion, twice Olympic silver medallist and Sydney 2000 Olympic champion. Her only defeats between 1991 and 2001 were in two Olympic finals.

Inspired by the exploits of Britain's Karen Briggs, Tamura first fought her in the 1990 Fukuoka Cup, a tournament that Briggs had won five times. Tamura stunned everyone by throwing Briggs for two waza-aris. A remarkable new talent had arrived. They met again in the 1991 world semi-final. This time Briggs was ready, turned her and pinned her for ippon. Tamura took home the bronze and did her homework on Briggs.

In the 1992 Olympic semi-final Tamura fought Briggs for the last time. Determined to stay out of newaza Tamura kept up a barrage of aggressive gripping and ashiwaza, dragging her veteran opponent around the mat, at one point partially dislocating the Briton's shoulder. Briggs re-set her shoulder, but was finally disqualified for passivity. In the final Tamura narrowly lost to Cecile Nowak (France) by two leg-grab kokas.

By the 1996 Olympics, Tamura was the number one player in the world. She had won two world titles, displaying superb technique. She was lightning fast and never gave up: in the final of the Makuhari world championships she produced a remarkable morote-gari ippon on her Chinese opponent in the very last second of the match! She had exceptional classical skills, from right-handed uchimata and osoto-gari, to efficient newaza, favouring hold-downs. Red-hot favourite for the Olympic title, she carried Japan's flag with pride at the opening ceremony.

She blitzed her way into the final, throwing everyone for ippon. But she met her match in the unknown 16 year old North Korean, Sun-Hui Kye, who refused to be overawed by Tamura, the crowd, or the occasion, and stopped everything thrown at her. With 30 seconds to go Tamura overstretched herself with an osoto-gari attack and Kye countered her for a koka, enough to prevent Tamura taking the title.

A four-year unbeaten run and two more world titles followed, equalling Karen Briggs' record. Only the Olympic title eluded her, and she went to Sydney knowing only gold would do. The atmosphere in the Convention Centre at Darling Harbour was unbelievable. There were so many Japanese flags, it was as if the whole country had come to support her!

Her form was not as sparkling as it was in Atlanta. She struggled to a yuko win over Zhao of China, but produced a beautiful right-handed oguruma ippon on Lusnikova (Ukraine), to reach the semi-final. With a forbidding sense of deja-vu, she faced another unknown young North Korean, Hyon-hyang Cha. Reluctant to attack, the first three minutes of the fight slipped away without score. With nothing to separate the two Tamura wound up the pace and the pressure, attacked and took the Korean into newaza. The last 30 seconds was non-stop aggression by Tamura, and on the bell, to the crowd's relief, she took the decision.

As Tamura stepped onto the mat for her third Olympic final against Lioubov Brouletova (Russia) a sea of Japanese flags and a wall of noise let her opponent know she had the crowd to beat as well as Tamura.

RYOKO TAMURA

DOB **6 September 1975**
COUNTRY **Japan**
WEIGHT **-48kg**
HEIGHT **1.45m 4ft 9ins**
OCCUPATION **Judoka**

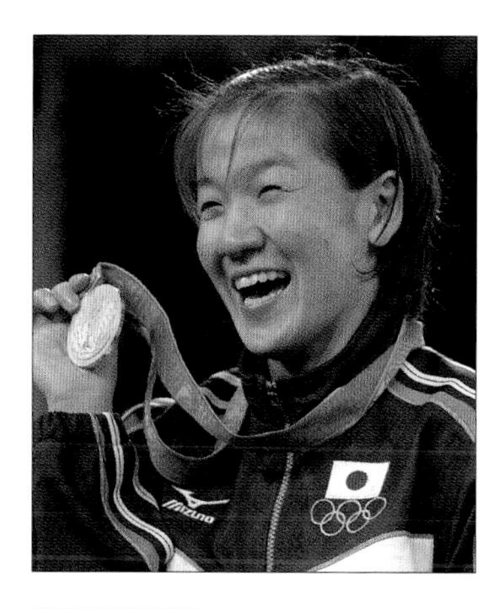

BEST RESULTS

Olympic Games
Barcelona 1992 silver
Atlanta 1996 silver
Sydney 2000 gold

World Championships
Barcelona 1991 bronze
Hamilton 1993 gold
Makuhari 1995 gold
Paris 1997 gold
Birmingham 1999 gold

Asian Games
Hiroshima 1994 gold

Asian Championships
Osaka 1991 bronze

Tournoi de Paris
1993 gold

Fukuoka Tournament
Gold: 1990, 1991, 1992, 1993, 1994, 1995, 1996, 1997, 1999, 1999, 2000

TECHNIQUES
Right osoto-gari, right uchimata, right seoi-otoshi, uchi-mata sukashi, right ouchi-gari, de-ashi-barai, morote-seoi-nage, yoko-shiho-gatame

Olympic Games final, Sydney 2000.
Versus Lioubov Brouletova (Russia).

It did not last long. With a superb piece of timing, Tamura rose to the occasion, darting underneath the Russian with a perfect right uchimata. The referee's arm shot into the air. It was third time lucky, and Olympic title was hers.

Asked what it was like to have finally taken the gold, she said: 'It's like meeting your first love again, after 80 years away.' She dedicated victory to her fans: 'This is not only my victory, but theirs as well. They gave me great encouragement, and their support brought me this medal.' For the Japanese nation there was elation and relief; the national heroine was finally, indisputably, one of the all time greatest champions of judo.

Olympic Games Quarter-Final, Sydney 2000. O-guruma ippon on Lusnikova (Ukraine).

KOSEI INOUE

DOB **15 May 1978**
TOWN/COUNTRY **Japan**
WEIGHT **-100kg**
HEIGHT **1.83m 6ft 0ins**
OCCUPATION **Judoka**

BEST RESULTS

Olympic Games
Sydney 2000 gold

World Championships
Birmingham 1999 gold

Asian Games
Bangkok 1998 gold

Tournoi de Paris
2000 gold

All Japan Championships
2000 silver (open)
2001 gold (open)

Japanese National Championships
1997 bronze
1998 silver
1999 gold

Hungarian Cup
2001 gold

FAVOURITE TECHNIQUES
Right uchimata, right ouchi-gari, right drop morote-seoinage, right osoto-gari

KOSEI INOUE is, at the time of writing, the superstar of the Japanese team. Japanese flag-bearer in Sydney he produced the most electrifying judo of the tournament, adding the Olympic title to his world title. Speaking after the Olympics, Nicolas Gill of Canada, the man he beat in the final, reputedly said: 'I am the champion of the world – because the guy that beat me is not of this world!'

Inoue combines strength with a remarkable speed and wastes no time in attacking: the instant he obtains his right-handed grip, he attacks – a direct uchimata being his tokui-waza. His first two fights in the Olympics lasted 18 and 9 seconds respectively. His fights are furious explosions of adrenalin that leave the spectator breathless with excitement. No one who saw it will forget the superb 1999 world final between Inoue and the Korean, Sung-ho Jang, in which either could have scored at any moment. An ouchi-gari from Inoue covered the whole mat, almost ending in the crowd. A counter of Jang's nearly caught the Japanese. Inoue won by yuko, but risked everything in an attempt to score ippon, even in the dying seconds of the match.

At the 2000 Tournoi de Paris, Inoue fought the veteran Frenchman Stephane Traineau in the final. Traineau had the whole crowd willing him to victory. Many fighters crack under this kind of pressure in France, but Inoue dropped under Traineau with a morote-seoi-nage to score ippon.

But all his previous victories paled into insignificance by comparison with the way in which he won the Olympic final. Nicolas Gill looked magnificent all day. The hard, experienced left-hander was determined to keep his right sleeve back and prevent Inoue's preferred grip. But eventually Inoue caught the sleeve and immediately feinted twice with ouchi-gari. On the second feint Gill froze. Inoue blasted in with uchimata, lifting the Canadian off his feet and spinning him over for an unforgettable ippon. Inoue was champion. On the podium he carried a photograph of his dead mother. His father had carried it throughout the day. Inoue had wanted her to witness his greatest day.

However he does have a bogey man. Antal Kovacs of Hungary was 1992 Olympic and 1993 world champion. Since then he has not been able to reach the same heights (though he won the 2001 Tournoi de Paris) but he beats Inoue. They fought in the Hungarian Cup in early 1999. Kovacs was the winner. He faced him again in the crucial fight of the match between Asia and Europe in the 2001 Millennium Cup. (Inoue was in fine form, having thrown everyone for ippon the previous day) In a moment of pure drama, the Hungarian threw Inoue for ippon with his own technique, right uchimata preceded by a couple of feints!

However Inoue then defeated world Open weight champion Shinichi Shinohara to win the 2001 All Japan title, the first non super heavyweight fighter to take the coveted trophy since 1974. It was a massive victory for him: 'The moment I learned I had won, all the strength left my body and I became light-headed,' he said afterwards. But it remains to be seen whether Kosei Inoue can become as great a champion as some of his predecessors. He is still young enough to break all the record books if he stays uninjured, as highly motivated and overcomes the rejuvenated Kovacs. If he does all that he could be the greatest champion of them all.

Olympic Games final, Sydney 2000. Versus Nicolas Gill (Canada).